D1486601

COOKING
THE JEWISH WAY

COOKING
THE JEWISH WAY

ANN WALD

SPRING BOOKS

SPRING BOOKS

SPRING HOUSE · SPRING PLACE · LONDON NW5

© *Books for Pleasure Ltd. 1961*

Printed in Czechoslovakia

T 828

WITH ACKNOWLEDGMENTS

AND THANKS TO MY SON DAVID

Contents

Introduction

Jewish cooking is recognised as being good cooking. It is cosmopolitan: it has adopted and adapted the best of many countries and peoples, adding it to a background peculiarly its own. Jewish people have always been noted for their home life, and no happy home is achieved without a good housewife, which means, among other things, a good cook.

Some of the recipes you will find in this book have been handed down through many generations; however, styles of cooking move with the times and I have included many recipes for modern living, that is, recipes which are simple and easy to prepare. A good cook can always elaborate on a simple recipe.:

None of the recipes you will find here are beyond the capabilities of the average cook. Some of them may appear to be unusual, but I am certain they are all worth a trial. Even the humble bread pudding, made to my recipe, is, although easy to prepare, excellent.

Jewish cooking is symbolised by the strict avoidance of mixing milk and meat and their products in the same dish, and in fact milk and meat dishes are never served at the same meal. In addition, certain foods are prohibited.

Only those animals that have the cloven hoof and chew the cud are permitted, and then only after humane ritual killing and further preparation (i. e. kashering).

Fish must have fins and scales.

Poultry is also killed according to Jewish humane ritual killing.

No bird of prey, no bird that is shot, and nothing that dies of itself is permitted.

These limitations, such as they are, do not mean that the Jewish diet is monotonous. Quite the contrary, and a glance through this book will soon dispel any such fears.

On the Jewish Festivals, it is usual to serve certain dishes that have become closely associated with those Festivals. That does not mean to say that these dishes are only prepared at these special times; most of them are, in fact, prepared throughout the year. Below I have listed the chief Festivals and customs at these times.

Finally, a few words to the cook! A good cook is clean, exact and never in too much of a hurry to get the dish done. It is the initial preparation, the blending of the right ingredients in their proper proportions that leads to results which are 'a joy to behold and a delight to eat'. If you put your whole heart and mind into your cooking, success is assured.

The Sabbath Day

The days are counted from sunset to sunset and the Sabbath commences at sunset on Friday and terminates at sunset on Saturday. In Jewish households, just prior to the commencement of the Sabbath, the table is laid especially. A white tablecloth, a minimum of two candles in candlesticks, two loaves of bread that are especially baked and shaped, salt and wine are placed on the table. The housewife when lighting the candles makes a special benediction over them. Before the evening meal, the master of the house makes a benediction over a glass of kosher wine (wine that is specially made for such purposes) of which all partake. He then makes a prayer over the loaves, from one of which he cuts a piece, dips it in the salt and then it is eaten.

THE JEWISH NEW YEAR *(Rosh Ha Shanah)* which occurs in September or early October calls for the traditional *Honey cake (Lekach)*.

EVE OF THE DAY OF ATONEMENT *(Erev Yom Kippur)* occurs on the evening previous to the Day of Atonement (the tenth day of the New Year) and is observed as a solemn Fast. The meal served might include *Kreplach* and *Tzimmis*.

THE HARVEST FESTIVAL *(Succoth)* commences four days after the Day of Atonement. *Stuffed cabbage* is usually an item on the menu.

THE FESTIVAL OF LIGHTS *(Chanukah)* occurs in December. *Latkes* are a 'must' for this Festival.

THE FEAST OF ESTHER *(Purim)*. This festival includes a period of fasting, followed by an especially nice meal. Purim takes place exactly four weeks before Passover. *Hamantaschen cakes* are definitely peculiar to this occasion.

THE PASSOVER *(Pesach)* is characterised by the eating of *Matzos* (unleavened bread) as all leaven is prohibited. Passover is a specia ised branch of Jewish cooking and is dealt with separately in this book (see page 183—195).

PENTECOST *(Shevuoth)* occurs seven weeks after Passover and it is usual to serve *Cheese cake* and Cheese blintzes on this Festival.

Useful Facts and Figures

COMPARISON OF ENGLISH
AND AMERICAN WEIGHTS AND MEASURES

English weights and measures have been used in most of the recipes in this book. The following table gives their conversion into cups and tablespoons. It should be remembered that the American pint equals 16 oz. whereas the Imperial pint used in Britain equals 20 oz. An American standard measuring cup holds 8 oz. or half an American pint. The American tablespoon is smaller than the English one, holding 3 teaspoonfuls, or roughly 1 rounded dessertspoonful.

Solid Measure

ENGLISH	AMERICAN
1 lb. Butter or other fat	2 cups
1 lb. Flour	4 cups
1 lb. Granulated or Castor Sugar	2 cups
1 lb. Brown (moist) Sugar	2⅔ cups
1 lb. Icing or Confectioner' Sugar	3 cups
1 lb. Syrup or Treacle	1 cup
1 lb. Rice	2 cups
1 lb. Dried Fruit	2 cups
1 lb. Chopped Meat (finely packed)	2 cups
1 lb. Lentils or Split Peas	2 cups
1 lb. Coffee (unground)	2⅓ cups
1 lb. Soft Breadcrumbs	4 cups
½ oz. Flour	1 level tablespoon
1 oz. Flour	1 heaped tablespoon
1 oz. Syrup or Treacle	1 tablespoon
1 oz. Sugar	1 level tablespoon
1 oz. Jam or Jelly	1 level tablespoon
½ oz. Butter	1 tablespoon smoothed off

FRENCH MEASURES

It is difficult to convert to French measurements with absolute accuracy, since 1 oz. is equivalent to 28.352 grammes. The table below is therefore very approximate.

Liquid Measure

Approximately 1¾ pints may be regarded as equal to 1 litre. 1 demilitre is half a litre, and 1 décilitre is one-tenth of a litre.

Solid Measure

1 oz. is equal to approximately 30 grammes.
Approximately 2 lb. 3 oz. is equal to 1 kilogramme.

COOKING TEMPERATURES

Water

Simmering 180 °F.
Boiling 212 °F.

Oven Temperatures	Electricity °F.	Gas Regulo No.	Gas °F.
COOL	225—250	0—½	225
VERY SLOW	250—275	½—1	250
SLOW	275—300	1—2	275
VERY MODERATE	300—350	2—3	300
MODERATE	375	4	350
MODERATELY HOT	375—400	5	375
HOT	400—450	6—7	400
VERY HOT	450—500	8—9	450

Note. This table is an approximate guide only. Different makes of cookers vary and if you are in any doubt about the setting it is as well to refer to the manufacturer's temperature chart.

To convert °F. to °C., subtract 32° and multiply by $\frac{5}{9}$.
To convert °C. to °F., multiply by $\frac{9}{5}$ and add 32°.

Some Useful Hints

TO MAKE BREADCRUMBS — Using a fine grater, rub down some stale bread or put through a mincer.

TO WEIGH GOLDEN SYRUP — The scales should be thickly dredged with flour before pouring in the syrup, which will then slip off the scales without sticking.

TO DISSOLVE GELATINE — Moisten the gelatine with *COLD* water and then stand container in saucepan of water. Heat gently, stirring until the gelatine is dissolved.

ORANGE AND LEMON JUICE — To ensure a greater amount of juice being extracted, immerse fruit in boiling water for a few minutes before squeezing.

TO CUT FRESH BREAD AND CAKES — The knife should be dipped in boiling water.

GLASS — A glass will not crack or break if a spoon is put in it before pouring in boiling liquid.

SALT — A few grains of rice put in the salt container will keep the salt from becoming damp.

FAT — When rendering fat, put a small piece of onion in the pan. This improves the flavour and keeping time.

FRUITS — When stewing acidy fruits, add a half teaspoon bicarbonate soda to each pound of fruit and less sugar will be required.

Cooking Terms

AU GRATIN — This term is applied to a dish which is covered with sauce, breadcrumbs and/or grated cheese. The dish is generally then browned under the grill or in the oven.

BASTING — To spoon fat or liquid over food during process of cooking to keep it moist.

BLANCH — Pour boiling water over the food and let it stand for 2 or 3 minutes, then drain.

BOUQUET GARNI — A bouquet of herbs, usually parsley, thyme, bay leaf, tied together and used to flavour sauces, stock, stews.

COURT BOUILLON — A liquid made from boiling water wine, vegetables, herbs and seasoning used for cooking fish.

CROQUETTES — Mixtures, generally of meat, fish or eggs, which have been dipped in egg and breadcrumbs and fried in deep fat.

CROUTONS — Very small pieces of bread, fried in butter or oil and served with soup.

CREAMING — To beat ingredients together until light and fluffy.

DREDGE — To lightly coat with sugar or flour.

FLAN — An open tart.

FOLDING IN — To combine two mixtures in such a way as to retain their lightness.

GLAZE — To brush pastry, pies, tarts, etc., with beaten egg or milk before cooking.

PUREE — To rub cooked fruit, vegetables or meat through a sieve to obtain a pulp.

ROUX — Flour cooked in hot melted fat and used as a base for thickening liquids, such as sauces, soups, stews.

RUBBING IN — Mixing flour and fat together with the fingertips to ensure lightness.

SAUTÉ — To brown in hot fat to desired requirements.

SIFT — To put dry ingredients through a fine sieve or sifter.

SIMMER — To cook in liquid that is kept just below boiling point.

HORS-D'OEUVRE

Hors-d'oeuvre usher in the meal and should be chosen with an eye to the main course. They are not meant to satisfy the appetite but really to heighten or incite it. They should be attractively served and where practicable placed on a bed of lettuce, decorated with chopped parsley, mustard and cress etc.

In Jewish households, hors-d'oeuvre made with fat, meat, liver etc. would only be served before a meal where meat or poultry follows because, as explained in the introduction, according to Jewish dietary laws, meat and milk dishes are not eaten at the same meal.

A platter or dishes of separate items can be placed on the table and each person can help himself to all or any of the items. These dishes make a very colourful display on the table and look most inviting.

CHOPPED HERRING

2 salt herrings (bought from
the barrelled salted herrings)
1 small Spanish onion
little white vinegar

1 large cooking apple
little granulated sugar
2 hard-boiled eggs

Soak herrings for at least 12 hours, changing water to get rid
of the salt. Skin, fillet and chop or put through a mincer with
all other ingredients, but keep one egg separate. Add vinegar
and sugar to individual taste. Garnish with the other egg,
chopped finely.

ROLLMOPS

4 salt herrings (bought from
the barrelled salted herrings)
2 large Spanish onions
white vinegar

½ lemon
few peppercorns and bay
leaves
2 lumps sugar

Soak the herrings for at least 12 hours, changing the water to
get rid of the salt. Remove the heads and split the herrings
down the centre and clean out. Place some very thinly sliced
onion on the herrings and roll up, starting at the head-end.
Secure with a cocktail stick or tie with some white cotton.
Place in a jar of cold water with the vinegar to taste (the water
should be very sharply flavoured), lemon cut into slices,
peppercorns, bay leaves, and the sugar.

The rollmops will be ready for eating in four or five days,
but they will keep well in the jar for at least 2 weeks.

PICKLED HERRINGS

The ingredients and method of pickling are exactly the same
as for Rollmops. The herrings after being washed are placed
whole in the jar and the onions thinly sliced and the other
ingredients placed between each herring.

SMOKED SALMON

Allow approximately 1 oz. per person

This is usually served with a wedge of lemon and accompanied by brown bread and butter. Garnish with slices of fresh cucumber when in season.

CHOPPED LIVER

4 oz. liver (preferably chicken)	2 hard-boiled eggs
1 large onion	1 tablespoon chicken fat

Peel and cut up onion finely and fry in fat until lightly browned; add liver, cut into thin slices, and cook until tender. Mince mixture with the eggs, season to taste and add enough of the fat left in the pan to make the mixture moist to the consistency of a pâté.

This is very nice served on water biscuits or small pieces of matzo with a little chopped parsley strewn on top.

EGG MAYONNAISE

For each person allow:

1 hard-boiled egg	some lettuce leaves
1 tomato	fresh cucumber slices
mayonnaise	(when in season)

Cut the hard-boiled egg lengthwise and place on lettuce leaves. Arrange the tomato and cucumber slices around and coat egg with mayonnaise.

This can be served as an hors-d'oeuvre as well as a luncheon or supper dish. When served as the latter, augment with anchovies, a sardine, a small quantity of potato and beetroot salad.

EGGS AND ONIONS

1 large Spanish onion *or*   2 hard-boiled eggs
1 bunch spring onions   1 tablespoon chicken fat

Chop peeled Spanish onion very finely (when using spring onions, snip with scissors into very small pieces). Mix with the grated eggs and the fat. Add salt to taste.

CREAM CHEESE AND APPLE

4 oz. cream cheese   2 tablespoons cream or top
1 sweet apple   milk

Peel and chop apple very finely and mix with the cheese and cream. Season with a little pepper and serve on cream cracker biscuits. A little paprika pepper shaken over the top looks very nice.

CREAM CHEESE AND NUTS

4 oz cream cheese   2 oz chopped nuts
2 tablespoons cream or top milk

Mix cheese with the nuts and bind well with the cream. Serve on cream cracker biscuits and sprinkle a little paprika pepper on top to add colour.

STUFFED TOMATOES

Allow to each person:

1 large firm tomato   cooked vegetables mixed
                             with mayonnaise

Cut the top off the tomato. Scoop out the seeds and fill with the vegetable filling. Place on a bed of lettuce with thin slices of fresh cucumber if desired.

MELON

1 melon   ground ginger
castor sugar

A melon is tested for ripeness by pressing the top of the fruit with the ball of the thumb. It should feel soft to the touch.

Melon should be served iced, wherever possible, in wedges (seeded), with castor sugar and ground ginger handed round separately.

GRAPEFRUIT

Allow ½ grapefruit per person   tinned cherries
sugar   little sherry

Prepare the grapefruit into sections in the shell. According to the acidity of the fruit, add sugar and a teaspoon of sherry. Place a cherry on top before serving. The grapefruit should be prepared several hours before serving to allow the fruit to marinate in the sugar and sherry.

FRUIT COCKTAIL

The combination for this should be according to one's own taste, but a few suggestions are listed here:

1. Mandarin oranges with small pieces of melon.
2. Pineapple pieces with pieces of pear, cherries, grapes.
3. Small fresh pineapple, cut lengthwise. Scoop out flesh, being careful not to break the skin. The flesh is cut up small and mixed with a tin of fruit cocktail and served in the shell.
4. Cut a small fresh pineapple lengthwise. Scoop out the flesh, cut into small pieces and place back in the shell.

SUGGESTIONS FOR A PLATTER OR SEPARATE DISHES OF HORS-D'OEUVRE

Arrange dishes of

diced cooked beetroot	cucumber slices (fresh or pickled)
anchovies	sardines
potato salad	vegetable salad
olives	chopped herring
pickled herring	small rolled pieces of smoked salmon
tomatoes	lettuce

Serve with a dish of salad cream or mayonnaise.

SOUPS AND GARNISHES

A good cook is known for the fine soups she produces. On a cold day there is nothing more acceptable than a plate of rich thick soup, while on a hot day a clear soup is most refreshing.

The basis of good tasty soup is naturally the liquid (known as stock) in which the ingredients are combined and it would not be amiss if one spent a little time in perfecting the art of stock making. So many different soups are made with the same stock (just by adding different garnishes and ingredients) that it is worth while to make a fairly large quantity of stock which will keep for a few days in the refrigerator. When a pressure cooker is used for making stock, the cooking time is greatly lessened.

For the purpose of Jewish cookery I have divided the soups into two sections, i. e. Meat Soups (Fleischig) which are eaten when meat dishes are served, and Vegetable and Cream Soups (Milchig) which are served with milk and or fish dishes, as Jewish dietary laws forbid the partaking of meat and milk dishes at the same meal.

MEAT SOUPS

BONE STOCK

2 shin bones	3 quarts cold water
some beef bones	1 dessertspoon salt
1 onion	1 carrot

The butcher will chop up the bones and when they are prepared for cooking (kashered, i. e. according to Jewish dietary laws) place them in a large saucepan with the cold water and salt. Bring to the boil and skim well.

Simmer gently for 3 hours then strain into a basin. When cold skim off all the fat that has risen to the top. Store and use as required.

MEAT STOCK

1 lb. shin of beef	2 quarts cold water
trimmings of meat from bones	1 onion
4 sticks celery	2 carrots
	salt and pepper to taste

Proceed as with BONE STOCK.

CONSOMMÉ

1 quart meat stock	2 sticks celery
1 egg white	1 carrot
shell of the egg	1 onion

Put the stock into a saucepan, add the egg white slightly beaten and the shell broken into small pieces. Whisk over gentle heat until it boils and boil for 3 minutes. Then simmer for 30 minutes. Skim and strain through fine muslin.

This process is known as clarifying stock, and the liquid we now have is Consommé or Clear Soup. By adding various garnishes we produce different soups, usually named after the garnish.

CONSOMMÉ JULIENNE

2 pints consommé   1 cooked leek
1 cooked carrot   1 cooked heart of celery
1 cooked turnip

Peel and cut vegetables into very thin strips. Add to the consommé and simmer for a few minutes.

CONSOMMÉ À L'ITALIENNE

2 pints consommé   small pieces of cooked macaroni *or*
a few cooked peas   small pieces of cooked spaghetti

Add ingredients to consommé and simmer for a few minutes.

CONSOMMÉ NIÇOIS

2 pints consommé   2 small tomatoes
some small pieces of cooked vermicelli
     (lockshen, see page 35)

Peel and cut tomatoes into small squares and add with the vermicelli to the consommé. Simmer for a few minutes.

CONSOMMÉ ROYALE

2 pints consommé   savoury custard (see page 31)

Cut up some savoury custard into tiny pieces. Place in the soup plate and add the hot consommé.

WHITE STEW

2 pints chicken soup
4 oz. minced beef or veal
(see *Chopmeat* page 71)

2 eggs
lemon juice

Make small balls of prepared minced meat and simmer in the soup for 15 minutes. Add lemon juice to taste and when cool beat some of the liquid into the well beaten eggs. Add rest of liquid and put back into saucepan to reheat. Stir continuously whilst reheating as eggs will curdle. Serve with a few of the meat balls and some cut up pieces of chicken giblet.

The soup will be much nicer if a little veal or some veal bones are cooked with the chicken when making the soup. This recipe has always been known as 'White Stew', although it is really a soup.

CHICKEN SOUP

1 boiling fowl
1 onion
2 carrots

3 sticks of celery
giblets, excluding the liver
salt and pepper

The chicken can be cut into the required number of serving pieces. Place them in a saucepan with 5 pints of cold water. Bring to the boil, skim and simmer for 30 minutes. Add the peeled vegetables and seasoning and simmer for a further 2 hours or until the chicken is tender. Remove chicken pieces and serve separately.

Chicken soup is invariably served with lockshen, kneidlech, kreplech (see pages 35, 37, 36).

LOCKSHEN SOUP

(Vermicelli)

To each plate of hot chicken soup, add one or two tablespoons of cooked lockshen, (see page 35) but the amount will depend on individual taste.

BARLEY SOUP (1)

1 quart stock
2 tablespoons medium barley
2 finely cubed carrots
a few mushrooms or
    mushroom stalks

1 onion, sliced
2 tomatoes, chopped
3 celery stalks, sliced
seasoning to taste

Put all ingredients in a large saucepan, bring to the boil and simer for 1 hour.

BARLEY SOUP (2)

Instead of using stock, this can be made with meat and/or chicken, in which case boil the meat with the vegetables. When using chicken, boil the required amount of chicken for about one hour, and proceed as for *Barley Soup (1)*.

OXTAIL SOUP

1 oxtail	2 tablespoons margarine
1 large onion	3 quarts cold water
1 carrot	seasoning
1 small tin tomato purée	

Melt the fat in a saucepan, add the sections of the oxtail and brown on all sides. Remove the sections from the pan, add vegetables and brown them in the same fat. Put the oxtail back, add water and tomato purée and bring to the boil. Skim well and simer for 4 hours. A little medium barley may be added 30 minutes before serving. Strain and remove all fat. Reheat and serve with small pieces of the meat, cut from the bones.

VEGETABLE AND CREAM SOUPS

VEGETABLE STOCK

This is made by combining a mixture of many kinds of root vegetables, e.g. celery, onions, leeks, potatoes, turnips, carrots. Peel and cut the vegetables into small pieces and place in cold water with salt to taste Allow 2 pints of water to every pound of vegetables, and simmer for about 1 hour. This stock should be used the same day as it is made.

MUSHROOM SOUP

2 pints stock	1 oz. fat or margarine
8 oz. mushrooms	seazonings
1 oz. flour	

Heat fat in saucepan and cook the washed, peeled and chopped mushrooms (including the finely chopped stalks) for a few minutes. Blend in flour, then stir in stock, stirring until it boils. Cook gently for 30 minutes. Season to taste.

CREAM OF MUSHROOM SOUP

1 lb. mushrooms	1 pint milk
1 small onion	2 oz. butter
2 pints vegetable stock or water	1 oz. flour

Melt 1 oz. butter in a saucepan and cook the finely cut up mushrooms and the onion until tender. Put through a sieve saving some pieces of the mushrooms. Make the sauce as directed for *Cream of Cauliflower Soup* (see page 30), add sieved vegetables and stock, season to taste and bring to the boil. Simmer for a few minutes, stirring continuously. Add pieces of mushroom and serve hot.

CREAM OF ASPARAGUS SOUP

Proceed as for *Cream of Mushroom Soup*, but substitute a small bundle of asparagus for the mushrooms.

The asparagus will be boiled until tender, and not sautéed.

CREAM OF POTATO SOUP

4 large peeled potatoes	2 oz. butter or margarine
2 leeks	1 oz. flour
2 pints water or vegetable stock	seasoning
1 pint milk	

Melt 1 oz. fat in a saucepan and gently fry potatoes and leeks which have been cut up very thinly. Add water or vegetable stock and simmer until potatoes are tender. Put the vegetables through a fine sieve and make the sauce as for *Cream of Cauliflower Soup* (see page 30). Add the sieved vegetables, the stock and simmer gently for 10 minutes, stirring continuously. Season to taste.

CREAM OF CAULIFLOWER SOUP

1 medium sized cauliflower
3 sticks celery
1 small onion
¾ pint milk

1½ pints water or vegetable
stock
1 oz. flour
1 oz. butter
seasoning

Cook cauliflower in the liquid with the finely chopped onion and diced celery. Put ingredients through a sieve, saving a few flowerettes for garnishing. While cauliflower is cooking, make a sauce as follows: stir the flour into the melted butter, then slowly add milk, stirring to keep smooth. Season. Add the purée and the water in which the vegetables were cooked. Serve hot with flowerettes.

CREAM OF TOMATO SOUP

2 pints water or vegetable stock
½ pint milk
2 lb. fresh or tinned tomatoes
little brown vinegar
seasoning

little sugar
1 oz. flour
1 oz. butter
1 tablespoon Worcester
sauce

Cook the tomatoes in the water or stock for 30 minutes and then put through a sieve. Make a roux in a saucepan with the fat and flour, stir in milk, bring to the boil and simmer for 5 minutes. Add the sieved tomatoes, the liquid in which they were cooked, sauce, vinegar and sugar to taste. Bring to the boil and simmer for 10 minutes, stirring continuously. A spoonful of cream put into each soup plate when serving the soup is a welcome addition.

CREAM OF ONION SOUP

4 large Spanish onions
2 pints water or vegetable stock
1½ pints milk
1 oz. flour

2 oz. butter
2 oz. Parmesan cheese
seasoning

Cook the peeled and finely chopped onions in 1 oz. of the fat until tender. Put through a sieve. Make a roux in saucepan with the remainder of fat and flour, add milk and stock, bring to the boil and simmer for a few minutes. Add the sieved onions and season to taste. Place a few croutons in each soup plate, pour over the hot soup and sprinkle 1 tablespoon Parmesan cheese on top.

PEA SOUP

8 oz. split peas
1 large carrot
1 onion
1 potato

1 small turnip
3 pints water or stock
salt and pepper

Simmer peas and the finely cut up or grated vegetables in the liquid until very soft, (approximately 2 hours). Put all through a sieve, return to saucepan, stir until boiling and season to taste.

LENTIL SOUP

This is made exactly like *Pea Soup*, but substitute lentils for the peas.

BORTSCH

(Beetroot Soup)

2 lb. raw red beetroots	2 eggs
2 tablespoons lemon juice	salt to taste
3 pints cold water	

Peel and cut beetroots very finely or put them through a mincer. Place them in a saucepan with the cold water and boil gently until tender. Strain and cool. Into the well beaten eggs add about half a pint of the liquid, stirring all the time. Gradually add the rest of the liquid, lemon juice (according to taste) and a little salt.

When served hot (and when heating, stir continuously to prevent the eggs from curdling), it is customary to place a hot boiled potato in the plate.

ONION SOUP

4 large Spanish onions	2 tablespoons margarine
4 pints stock	1 oz. flour
	seasoning

Peel and cut onions very finely and cook until golden brown in the hot melted fat in a saucepan. Blend in flour and cook for 2 or 3 minutes. Stir in stock and simmer for 40 minutes. Put all through a sieve, season to taste and serve boiling hot.

This soup is especially nice when served with croutons (see page 35).

POTATO SOUP

2 lb. boiled potatoes   2 quarts water or stock
1 large onion   1 oz. flour
1 oz. margarine   seasoning

Cook the peeled and chopped onion in the fat for 3 minutes and add flour. Mix well, stir in the stock and add the potatoes. Press all through a sieve and return to saucepan. Season to taste and simmer for 5 minutes. Serve with a little chopped parsley and a few croutons.

MINESTRONE SOUP

4 pints stock   1 carrot
heart of a small cabbage   1 onion
8 oz. tomatoes (fresh or   1 tablespoon rice
    tinned)   2 oz. macaroni
3 sticks celery   2 tablespoons margarine
1 turnip   seasoning

Shred the cabbage and cut the vegetables very finely. Cook all together in a saucepan in the melted fat over gentle heat for 5 minutes. Add stock, tomatoes, macaroni, rice and cook gently for one hour. Season to taste.

This is an excellent soup for cold weather and very satisfying.

CABBAGE SOUP

1 quart stock or water
1 small white cabbage
juice of 1 lemon
1 onion

1 pint tomato juice
2 large cooking apples
2 oz. sultanas or seedless
  raisins
little sugar

Discard outer leaves of cabbage and shred cabbage finely. Peel and grate apples and onions and put with cabbage in saucepan with stock or water, tomato juice and sultanas. Simmer for 40 minutes and then add lemon juice and sugar to taste.

CURRIED VEGETABLE SOUP

2 carrots
1 onion
1 potato
small tin tomato
  purée

2 pints stock
1 oz. margarine
1 teaspoon curry powder
  (or more according to taste)
a little salt

Prepare the vegetables and put through mincer. Melt the fat in a saucepan, add vegetables, curry powder and tomato purée. Cook slowly for 5 minutes, stirring well. Add stock and simmer for 30 minutes.

This is really a delicious soup and when well made will enhance the cook's reputation for soup making! Incidentally, it is also my favourite soup.

GARNISHES

A soup frequently derives its name from the garnish used. A little chopped parsley placed on top of meat or chicken soup when served looks very attractive.

CROÛTONS

Fry very small pieces of crustless bread in hot fat or margarine until golden brown, or they can be sautéd in a little fat or margarine.

EGG BALLS

2 hard-boiled eggs   seasoning
1 raw egg yolk

Press the hard boiled eggs through a sieve. Add seasoning and bind with the raw egg yolk. Roll into small balls and cook gently in boiling salted water for 5 minutes.

These can be added to any clear soup.

LOCKSHEN (VERMICELLI)

1 egg   little salt
4 oz. flour

Beat egg with a little salt. Add enough flour to make a fairly stiff dough. Knead well and roll out very thinly into a circle and leave to dry. Roll into 2 inch widths and cut very finely on a board into strips. Toss with the fingers to separate and spread out to dry. When quite dry boil slowly in salted water for 10 minutes, and strain.

FARFEL

Make the dough as for Lockshen (see page 35) but making sure that the dough is really stiff. Grate coarsely and separate for drying. When dry, boil in salted water for 5 minutes, drain through a colander and serve as a garnish for hot chicken soup.

The farfel can also be baked in a tin in a moderate oven. The pieces should be separated in the course of the baking. They should be well browned and then cooked as above, but for 10 minutes. The baked farfel is also a garnish for hot chicken soup or can be used as a vegetable when serving meat with gravy.

KREPLACH (RAVIOLI)

dough as for *Lockshen* (see page 35).

Filling

8 oz. of any cooked meat	seasoning
1 egg	1 little onion

Roll the dough out thinly and cut into 2 inch squares. Mince the meat and add a little chopped onion, salt and pepper and bind with a raw egg. Place 1 large teaspoon of the meat mixture into each square and fold opposite corners together to form a triangle, taking great care that the edges are well pressed together. Leave to dry for 30 minutes, then drop gently in boiling salted water and simmer for 15 minutes.

As well as being served with chicken soup, kreplach can be served with tomato sauce as a separate item in the menu.

KNEIDLECH (MATZO KLEIS)

5 heaped tablespoons medium matzo meal	1 egg
8 tablespoons boiling water	1 tablespoon chicken fat
	salt and pepper

Place meal in a bowl and pour on the boiling water. Add well beaten egg, seasoning and fat and mix thoroughly. The mixture should be rather firm (but NOT too firm) and a little more meal may be added if necessary.

With wet hands roll into small balls and cook gently in salted boiling water for 6 minutes. These are served with chicken soup and when made properly are tasty and very sponge-like.

They are also the garnish used in chicken soup during the Passover Festival when other garnishes made with cereals or flour are prohibited.

SAVOURY OR ROYALE CUSTARD

2 eggs	little seasoning
½ pint clear stock	

Beat the eggs well and add to the stock with a little seasoning. Pour into an ovenproof dish and place dish in a baking tin half-filled with cold water. Bake in a pre-heated moderate oven for 35 minutes until the custard is set. Leave until cold, turn out and cut into small pieces. Serve as a garnish in clear soup.

BOILED RICE

6 oz. long grained rice   salt
3 quarts boiling water

Scald the rice, then place in a bowl and wash with cold water. Place the rice in boiling water and boil slowly for 20 minutes, stirring occasionally. Add 2 or 3 teaspoons salt and strain through a colander. Pour boiling water through to separate the grains and steam to re-heat. Boiled rice is especially nice served in a plate of hot tomato or chicken soup.

Except for rice puddings, always use the long-grained rice.

Fish may be served either as the main course of a meal or as a subsidiary item on the menu. It is a good substitute for meat and is frequently served, one way or another, in Jewish households for the Sabbath. Some of the specialities are Sweet and Sour Fish, Gefillte Fish, Fresh Water Fish, Fried Fish.

When buying fish, make sure it is perfectly fresh - the flesh should be firm, the gills red and the eyes bright. Fresh fish has NO smell. Your fishmonger should always skin and fillet the fish as required.

There are five main ways of cooking fish - boiling, baking, grilling, frying and steaming. The fish should be well washed cut into suitably sized pieces and slightly salted before cooking.

BOILING. This method is used for large pieces of fish or small whole fish. Place the fish in boiling water or Court-bouillon (see page 41) and simmer until tender. Do not over-cook, as the fish will fall to pieces and will be flavourless.

BAKING. Place the fish in a greased dish, dot with butter or margarine and bake in a moderate oven, basting frequently. Cooking time about 30 minutes.

GRILLING. Place the fish under a hot grill. Cook on both sides for a few minutes according to thickness of fish. The fish should be basted with melted butter or margarine.

FRYING. Place the cleaned, washed and salted fish in a strainer. Beat up in a dish one or more eggs according to amount of fish to be fried. Put some flour or fine matzo meal on a plate. Half-fill a deep pan with oil and heat until VERY HOT. Wipe the pieces of fish with a clean cloth, dip into the flour or meal and then into the egg. Slip carefully into the hot oil and cook on both sides until nicely browned. Lift out carefully and drain well on white kitchen paper.

Note. Never put too many pieces of fish in the pan at the same time as this will cool the oil. Do not disturb the fish until it is ready for turning as otherwise it will break.

STEAMING. When properly steamed, the fish will be very appetising. It is recommended for serving to children and invalids. Place the fish in a soup plate, dot with a little butter or margarine and add a little milk. Cover with another plate and place on top of a saucepan of fast boiling water and steam until fish is cooked.

Haddock, plaice, sole or cod are best for steaming.

For sauces to be served with fish, see Savoury Sauces, pages 104 to 110.

COURT-BOUILLON
(Stock for boiling fish)

2 quarts water   1 bay leaf
2 onions   ½ teacup lemon juice *or*
2 carrots   wine vinegar
a few peppercorns

Wash and cut up vegetables and simmer with all other ingredients in the water. Strain before using. Cooking time, 1 hour.

BLOATERS

Allow one or two to each person as required.

Remove the head and split the fish down the back and remove the centre bone. Bloaters are nicest fried in butter or grilled. To fry, use only a small amount of butter or margarine and cook over a gentle heat. To grill, place the fish on a hot grill and cook on both sides.

CARP

Carp are fresh-water fish. They are in season from September until March. They are nicest when plain boiled as for sea bream. The liquid in which the fish is cooked will jelly when cold.

PLAICE

This fish lends itself to any of the methods given for cooking fish. Small plaice called 'flounders' can be cooked whole or filleted. The larger sized fish are usually cut across into slices. Steamed or grilled plaice is usually given to children and invalids as it is of very soft texture.

COD

Cod can be cooked by any of the methods listed previously.

COD WITH PARSLEY SAUCE

4 cod steaks	seasoning
4 oz. mushrooms	milk
	parsley sauce (see page 106)

Place the seasoned fish in a baking dish together with the chopped mushrooms, seasoning and milk. Cover with greaseproof paper and cook until fish is tender. Serve with parsley sauce.

COD AU GRATIN

4 cod steaks	grated cheese
1 oz. butter	seasoning
breadcrumbs	Mornay sauce (see page 105)
hot mashed potatoes	

Boil the fish gently in slightly salted water and when cooked place in an ovenproof dish. Cover with breadcrumbs and cheese sauce and bake in a moderate oven for 15 minutes. Pipe a border of mashed potato round the edge of the serving dish.

FRIED HERRINGS

Remove heads from required number of herrings. Clean and salt slightly and split if desired. Fry according to directions for frying fish at the beginning of this section.

SOUSED HERRINGS

4 herrings	water
brown vinegar	4 bay leaves
	12 peppercorns

Remove heads and clean fish, but do not split. Salt slightly. Place in a fireproof dish, cover with equal quantity of vinegar and water and add the spices. Bake in a moderately slow oven for 25 minutes.

POACHED HALIBUT WITH MUSHROOMS AND TOMATOES

4 serving pieces of halibut	a little milk
4 tomatoes	a little butter or
4 mushrooms	margarine
mashed potatoes	seasoning

Poach the halibut in a little milk until tender. Grill the mushrooms and the tomatoes cut in halves crossways. Place the fish down the centre of a serving dish and place a mushroom and two halves of the tomato on each piece. Surround with a piped border of mashed potato.

HALIBUT WITH TOMATOES AND POTATOES

4 serving pieces of halibut	1 small onion
1 oz. butter or margarine	4 potatoes baked in
4 peeled tomatoes	their jackets

Grill the fish and place in a warm oven to keep hot. Fry the peeled and finely cut up onion in the fat, add tomatoes. Serve the fish with a topping of this mixture and with a hot baked potato cut in half lengthwise dotted with butter or margarine.

SWEET AND SOUR HALIBUT
(with Béchamel Egg Sauce)

4 serving pieces of halibut   juice of 2 lemons
1 small onion   2 eggs
seasoning   ½ pint water
2 pieces lump sugar

Boil the peeled and sliced onion in water for 3 or 4 minutes.
Add washed and salted fish, seasoning, lemon juice and sugar.
Simmer for 30 minutes and adjust seasoning. Lift fish carefully into a dish. Strain the fish stock, cool and stir into well
beaten eggs. Return to the saucepan, simmer very slowly until
thickened, stirring continuously. Pour around the fish. This
is nicest eaten cold.

SWEET AND SOUR MACKEREL

2 mackerel cut into four pieces

Proceed exactly as with *Sweet and Sour Halibut*.

FRIED MACKEREL

2 large mackerel   wedges of lemon

Remove the heads, wash and completely split the fish down
the back and remove the centre bone. Salt, drain and fry
according to instructions for frying fish. Serve with wedges
of lemon.

GRILLED MACKEREL

2 large mackerel	a little chopped
a little butter or	parsley
margarine	wedges of lemon
seasoning	

Remove heads and split down the back. Wash and season well. Dot with fat and place under hot grill and cook until nicely browned. Serve with wedges of lemon and a little chopped parsley strewn on top of fish.

FRIED COD'S ROE

The roe should be washed and tied in a muslin bag and boiled in salted water for 15 minutes. Remove the roe and when cold cut it into thick slices and fry according to directions for frying fish (see page 40).

SEA BREAM

1 bream	water
1 onion	salt and pepper

This is a very scaly fish and it is advisable to ask the fishmonger to thoroughly prepare the fish for cooking. Wash well. Peel and chop the onion and add to water in a large saucepan, add salt and pepper and bring to boil. Put in the fish, which should be just covered with water, bring to boil and simmer gently for 30 minutes.

SOLES

Soles can be cooked by any of the methods listed for fish cookery, but perhaps the sole lends itself best to various garnishes and sauces as it is the most popular fish for luncheon and dinner parties.

I find that it is best to use the whole fish in the following recipes. Table size soles are generally 8 to 10 oz. each, and they should always be skinned on both sides.

FRIED SOLE

4 soles
wedges of lemon

tartare sauce (see page 110)

Prepare and fry soles according to the directions for frying fish (see page 40). Serve with tartare sauce and wedges of lemon.

SOLE MORNAY

4 soles
seasoning
very small onion

milk
Mornay sauce
(see page 105)

Place the prepared and seasoned soles in a baking dish, add milk just to cover them and the peeled onion cut very finely. Cook in a moderate oven until fish is tender. Lift on to a serving dish, cover with the sauce, sprinkle a little grated cheese on top and glaze under a grill. Use the strained liquid from the pan to make the sauce.

SOLE CAPRICE

4 soles	1 oz. flour
1 tablespoon chutney	3 oz. butter
seasoning	4 bananas

Prepare and fry soles as in *Sole Meuniere* (see page 48). While the fish are cooking, peel and cut bananas lengthwise and fry in another pan in butter, turning to cook evenly. When cooked, remove fish to a heated serving dish and keep hot. Arrange fried bananas round them. Blend chutney into butter remaining in pan and heat. Pour this chutney butter mixture over fish and bananas and serve at once.

SOLE PALACE

4 soles	12 heads asparagus (tinned)
4 oz. mushrooms	seasoning
4 tomatoes	1 oz. butter

Prepare and cook fish as for *Bonne Femme* (see page 49), but during cooking time fry the peeled mushrooms and tomatoes in the butter. Place cooked fish on a serving dish, arrange asparagus, mushrooms and tomaoes alternately down the fish and coat with the same sauce as for *Bonne Femme*.

SOLE VÉRONIQUE

4 soles
1 small onion, sliced thin
8 oz. seeded white grapes

1 glass white wine
water
seasoning
Béchamel sauce
(see page 105)

Place the prepared soles in an ovenproof dish and cover with a mixture of wine and water. Add onion and seasoning and cook in a fairly slow oven until tender. In the meantime place grapes in a saucepan with 1 tablespoon wine and heat until hot. Make sauce using strained liquid in which fish was cooked. Place fish on serving dish, surround with the grapes and coat with sauce.

SOLE MEUNIÈRE

4 soles
seasoning
2 oz. butter

lemon juice
1 oz. flour

Prepare the fish. Melt butter in a thick frying pan and when hot put in the sole which has been rolled in the flour (season this with salt and pepper). Cook over a medium heat until golden brown, turning to brown, on both sides. Lift out fish and keep hot. Cook the butter until it is dark brown, but be careful it does not burn, add lemon juice and pour over fish. Serve with wedges of lemon.

SOLE BONNE FEMME

4 soles	2 egg yolks
4 oz. mushrooms	1 oz. butter
1 glass white wine	milk
seasoning	

Place the prepared and seasoned soles in an oven dish. Add wine and enough milk to cover. Place a lid on the dish and cook in a moderate oven until fish are tender. Lift out and keep hot. In the meantime fry the peeled whole mushrooms in the butter. Drain the liquid from the casserole into a saucepan, add the well beaten yolks and stir continuously over a very low heat until thickened. Season to taste. Place the fish on a serving dish, the mushrooms down the centre of the fish, and mask with the sauce.

SMOKED HADDOCK WITH POACHED EGG

1 smoked haddock (about 1½ lb.)	a little butter
4 eggs	

Wash and trim the fish and cut into serving pieces. Place in a saucepan of boiling water and simmer for 10 minutes. Poach the eggs. Lift out the fish carefully with a perforated slice and serve each piece with melted butter and topped with a poached egg.

GEFILLTE FISH

Gefillte fish is a combination of two or three kinds of suitable fish, minced together with the appropriate ingredients. The mixture can be boiled or fried.

Some suggested combinations

haddock, cod, whiting, halibut
or haddock, sea bream, mackerel
or haddock, halibut and cod
or fresh water bream, pike, a little carp

2 onions	2 eggs
2 carrots	4 tablespoons medium
salt and pepper	matzo meal

The fishmonger will skin and fillet the fish, but save the bones and the skin for the stock. Wash and salt well and put the bones and skins in a saucepan with 2 pints of cold water and simmer whilst preparing the fish.

Mince together the fish, and the peeled onions, add the matzo meal, salt and pepper to taste and the well beaten eggs. With wet hands form into smooth pieces.

Strain the stock and discard the skins and bones. Return the stock to the saucepan with the sliced carrots, add the fish and boil gently for 1½ hours. Lift out carefully and place a slice of carrot on each piece of fish. This is best eaten cold with the stock served separately, and horseradish sauce is generally taken.

FRIED GEFILLTE FISH

The mixture and method are the same as the previous recipe, but form the mixture into patties. Dip them into fine matzo meal or flour and then in beaten egg and fry in hot oil on both sides until nicely browned.

SALMON

I suppose you would call salmon the 'King of fish'; it certainly is the most expensive. Scotch salmon is considered the best, particularly those from the River Tay, which after catching are marked on the head with the word 'Tay'. Salmon from Ireland is also good, with a fine flavour. The season usually opens the first week of February, and ends about July.

Salmon should be prepared very simply to preserve its flavour, and needs no sauces or fancy cooking, but you may like to try the following dishes.

PICKLED SALMON

4 small slices salmon	seasoning
1 small onion	2 bay leaves
white vinegar	6 peppercorns
1 pint water	

Peel and cut onion finely and boil in water for a few minutes. Prepare fish and place in boiling liquid, add seasoning, bay leaves and peppercorns and boil gently for 30 minutes. Lift out gently and place in a rather deep dish. Add vinegar to the liquid (it should be rather sharp to the taste) and pour it over the fish. Leave until cold.

If the fish is placed in a square of muslin in the saucepan, it can be lifted from the pan without breaking when it is cooked.

SWEET AND SOUR SALMON

This is prepared exactly like *Sweet and Sour Halibut* (see page 44). Serve the salmon cold with green salad and fresh cucumber.

BOILED SALMON

2 large slices	1 small onion
(cut in halves) *or*	seasoning
4 small slices	1 pint water

Cut the peeled onion finely and boil in water for a few minutes. Add the washed and salted fish, season, and boil very gently for 25 minutes. Lift out gently with a slice and serve with fresh green cucumber and mayonnaise sauce. Boiled salmon can be eaten hot or cold.

Since we have all become vitamin conscious, vegetables have become an essential item in our diet. Only very fresh vegetables should be purchased and should be cooked the same day. This will conserve their flavour and give the maximum nutrition. Vegetables should be cooked in very little water, and the salt added when almost cooked.

Never overcook
To preserve the bright green colour of certain vegetables, cook in an uncovered saucepan. It is wrong to add bicarbonate of soda to retain the colour as this destroys the vitamins.

Save the liquid in which vegetables have been cooked for making soups, sauces and vegetable stock.

Typical of Jewish dishes and strongly recommended are *Tzimmis* (page 60) and *Latkes* (page 57).

ASPARAGUS

Allow 6 heads per person

Cut off lower ends of stalks. Tie in small bundles and soak in lukewarm water for 5 minutes. Place in a pan of boiling water so that the asparagus lies absolutely flat so as not to break the delicate heads. Boil gently for about 20 minutes, add salt to taste just before end of cooking time. Drain well and serve with mayonnaise or hollandaise sauce (see pages 110, 107).

ARTICHOKES (FRENCH OR GLOBE)

1 artichoke per person

Choose plump and globular artichokes which should be of a good green colour. The most popular way of serving them is boiled and served with mayonnaise or French dressing.

Wash well, and place compactly in a saucepan. Cover with salted boiling water and cook gently for 25 minutes, keeping the saucepan covered. Drain and serve hot or cold.

To Eat. The leaves are removed one by one with the fingers and the base dipped in the dressing. This fleshy base is the part eaten. There is a cone of tender compact leaves in the centre of the artichoke. When lifted they reveal a fuzzy portion. This is lifted out and discarded and the remainder of the artichoke eaten.

AUBERGINES OR EGGPLANT

2 aubergines
butter, margarine or fat
  (for frying)

small clove garlic
(optional)

Peel and slice aubergines into ¼-inch slices and sprinkle with salt and the crushed clove of garlic. Leave for 30 minutes, then drain well. Fry in hot fat slowly until crisp and brown. The slices may be dipped in egg and breadcrumbs before frying.

CELERY

Celery can be eaten raw or cooked. It is invaluable for flavouring soups and stews. When raw, it is used for salads; young inner stalks are cut into 2-inch pieces and filled with cream cheese or it can be grated and served with the hors-d'oeuvre.

BRAISED CELERY

1 head of firm celery

seasoning
little butter or margarine

Clean and remove outer stalks and green leaves. (Save these for adding to soups.) Cut into 3 or 4 pieces according to size and wash very thoroughly. The celery can be cooked in the dish where meat is being roasted or laid in a well greased shallow oven dish, seasoned with salt and a little lemon juice. Pour some stock into the pan, dot with butter or margarine and bake in a moderate oven for 35 minutes.

POTATO PUFFS

 4 large potatoes, well scrubbed   seasoning
 2 tablespoons butter or margarine 2 egg whites

Bake the potatoes in their jackets. When tender, carefully cut in half lengthwise and scoop out the flesh. Cream this with the fat and seasonings and fold in the stiffly beaten egg whites. Fill the empty shells two thirds full of the mixture and return to a moderate oven for 15 minutes.

BOILED POTATOES

Old potatoes, after peeling, should be put into cold salted water, brought to the boil and cooked until tender (about 20 minutes).

New potatoes, after scraping, should be put into boiling salted water with a spring or two of mint and cooked until tender (about 15 minutes).

Peeled potatoes should be immediately placed in cold water to prevent discolouration.

ROAST POTATOES

 medium sized potatoes   fat for roasting
 seasoning

Peel and place potatoes in boiling water for 2 or 3 minutes. (This ensures a crisp roast potato.) Drain and place potatoes in a dish with hot melted fat, or round roasting meat. Roast in a moderate to hot oven.

POTATO PANCAKES (LATKES)

2 lb. potatoes	1 egg
2 tablespoons self-raising flour	seasoning
	oil for frying

Peel and finely grate the potatoes into a bowl of cold water and then strain through a muslin bag. Place the strained potatoes in a bowl, add the flour, salt and the egg well beaten. Mix thoroughly. Drop tablespoons of the mixture into hot oil and fry on both sides until nicely brown.

The secret of successful *latkes* is to ensure that all excessive liquid is drained from the grated potatoes.

STUFFED POTATOES

4 large potatoes, well scrubbed	seasoning
2 tablespoons butter or margarine	2 tablespoons grated cheese

Bake potatoes in their jackets. When tender, carefully cut down lengthwise in half, scoop out the flesh and cream it with the butter and seasoning. Add cheese and a little milk. Refill the potato shells and return to oven for 10 minutes.

BRUSSELS SPROUTS

Allow 4 to 6 Brussels sprouts per person	salt

Remove any discoloured leaves. Make a cut at the bottom of the sprout, wash and leave to soak in salted cold water for 20 minutes. Drain, wash, and cook in gently boiling salted water for 10 minutes. Do not overcook.

GREEN PEAS

Shell and place in boiling salted water to which a lump of sugar and a sprig or two of mint has been added. Simmer gently until peas are tender (about 15 minutes). Drain and serve with a knob of butter or margarine.

SPINACH

2 lb. spinach   salt

Choose crisp spinach. Wash in several waters until it is absolutely free from sand and grit. Place spinach in a saucepan with only the water that clings to the leaves, add a little salt and cook gently until tender, about 15 minutes. Drain well, chop finely or rub through a sieve.

Spinach is very nice topped with a poached egg.

CORN ON THE COB

Allow 1 corn cob per person   butter or margarine
salt

Free the corn from the husks and the silk. Put the corn into fast boiling salted water, making sure they are lying flat and completely imersed. Boil gently for 20 minutes. Drain and serve with melted butter or margarine. Overcooking will spoil the flavour of the corn.

BEANS (FRENCH AND RUNNER)

Cut ends off the beans and remove 'strings' from both sides. French beans need only be broken into 2 or 3 pieces and boiled in salted water for 15 minutes.

Runner beans should be sliced finely and cooked as above.

STUFFED CABBAGE

large white cabbage leaves
1 teacup cooked rice
1 lb. raw minced beef
1 small onion grated
salt and pepper

1 small tin tomatoes or tomato
  purée
2 oz. seedless raisins or sultanas
2 tablespoons brown sugar
a little water
lemon juice

Scald the leaves with boiling water and leave for 5 minutes to soften, and then drain. Mix the rice, meat, onion, salt and pepper well together and place 2 large tablespoons of the mixture in the centre of each leaf. Roll up like a parcel and tie securely with white thread; line a large saucepan with several cabbage leaves and place the rolls on top; add the purée, water, raisins, sugar and cover tightly. Cook gently for at least 2 hours, making sure there is liquid in the pan the whole time, adding a little more water if necessary. Add lemon juice and brown sugar according to taste.

CARROT TZIMMIS

1 lb. not too lean meat	2 oz. brown sugar
1 lb. carrots	dumpling (see page 90)
seasonings	

Place meat in a saucepan, cover with cold water and simmer until nearly tender. Wash, scrape and dice the carrots and add to meat, season, add sugar and simmer until meat and vegetables are really tender. The liquid will be practically absorbed. 30 minutes before end of cooking time add the dumpling.

During the past few years when people have become 'figure conscious' and have taken great note of vitamins, calories, etc., salads have played an important part in the diet. They can be served as a complement to another dish or can be served as the main course of a meal. They can be made from one ingredient or a combination of many, such as cooked or uncooked fruits, vegetables, etc.

Lettuce and watercress must be served crisp and cold and dressed just before serving. Separate leaves from lettuce heads, wash in several waters, as cold as possible, shake well and put in refrigerator in a plastic bag until ready for use.

TOMATO SALAD

tomatoes   dressing
lettuce

Select very firm ripe tomatoes. Peel and cut into thick slices or wedges and place on lettuce leaves. Serve with French dressing.

To skin tomatoes, immerse in boiling water for 2 minutes and the skin will come off easily.

Or place tomato on a fork over a flame. The skin will crack and it can then be easily removed.

STUFFED TOMATOES

Cut a slice from the stem end of each tomato.

Hollow out tomatoes and sprinkle insides with salt. Invert them to allow for draining and then chill.

Any of the following can be used as fillings according to the dish accompanying the salad:

Cole slaw, Russian salad, cream cheese, mixture of chopped celery and apple, chopped nuts, etc.

MIXED SALAD

Line a salad bowl with prepared lettuce. Add all or some of the following, arranged as attractively as possible:

Sliced cucumbers, tomatoes cut in slices or wedges, slices of hard-boiled egg, radishes, anchovies, some spring onions if desired.

Dress, or hand round dressing.

CUCUMBER AND PINEAPPLE SALAD

Arrange slices of cucumber on rings of tinned pineapple. Dress with French or mayonnaise dressing (see page 110) and serve.

CUCUMBER SALAD

Cut peel from a cucumber in strips. Slice, season with salt and chill.

Place slices on lettuce leaves, dress with desired dressing and serve immediately.

COLE SLAW

This is an American recipe which has become very popular in other countries. It is very appetising and can be eaten with fish or meat equally well.

1 small head of white cabbage	peeled and grated carrot
French dressing (see page 110)	sweet apple (optional)

Remove core and outer leaves of cabbage. Wash and dry well, shred very finely and chill. Add other ingredients and mix thoroughly with the dressing.

AVOCADO SALAD

Peel and slice lengthwise required number of Avocados and serve on lettuce leaves.

This salad may be augmented with peeled and pitted sections of orange and grapefruit.

Serve with French dressing.

RUSSIAN SALAD

This is a combination of cooked vegetables, diced, seasoned and mixed with mayonnaise to form a creamy mixture. Green peas, carrots, potato, small pieces of cauliflower, and French beans can be used. Place in salad bowl and serve.

LETTUCE, EGG AND ANCHOVY SALAD

1 head lettuce
2 hard boiled eggs

4 prepared anchovies
French dressin (see page 110)

Place prepared lettuce in a bowl. Add shelled and sliced eggs and decorate with the cleaned anchovies split in halves. Add dressing and serve immediately.

POTATO SALAD (1)

Dice 2 cups cooked cold potatoes and add two shelled and chopped hard-boiled eggs, 1 cup peeled and chopped onion and a little chopped celery. Season with salt and a very little pepper. Add ½ cup salad dressing, mix well, and place in a salad bowl.

Garnish with paprika pepper and sprigs of watercress.

POTATO SALAD (2)

Boil 8 small potatoes in their jackets. When tender, and while still hot, peel and slice them finely, mix with little grated onion, and season well with salt and pepper. Add salad dressing and garnish to taste.

GREEN PEPPER AND CHEESE SALAD

2 green peppers
4 oz. cream chesee

4 tablespoons cream

Wash peppers, cut off tops and scoop out all seeds. Mix cheese with cream and stuff peppers with this mixture. Place in refrigerator for 2 or 3 hours. Cut peppers into slices (not too thin) and serve on lettuce. Hand round mayonnaise.

The housewife who adheres to the Jewish dietary laws may feel herself a bit limited as to variety. But I think that not enough advantage is taken of the different ways in which the cheaper cuts of meat can be used, and a little ingenuity can produce some very successful and tasty dishes.

Only those animals that chew the cud and have the cloven hoof are permitted and of these only the forequarters, plus liver, tongue, heart, brains and sweetbreads are used.

All meat, poultry and offal are kashered, i. e. placed in a pan (especially used for this purpose only) containing cold water, completely covered with cold water and left for 30 minutes. The meat is then taken out, washed and profusely sprinkled on all sides with salt and put on a slatted board in a slanting position. After one hour, wash the meat under running cold water to free it from the salt, place in a pan of clean cold water, take out and again wash under running cold water. It is now kashered and ready for cooking.

Liver is washed, salted, held over a flame to sear it and then well washed.

TO COOK MEAT

BAKING. The seasoned meat is generally placed with a peeled, sliced onion and some water in the baking dish. Proceed as for roasting.

BRAISING. This method is used for the less tender cuts of meat. Dredge the meat with flour and brown on all sides in hot fat in a saucepan. Pour off excess fat, add about 1 pint stock or water and simmer until tender. Peeled and sliced onions, carrots and tomatoes may be added halfway during cooking time and greatly improve the dish.

FRYING. This method is used for chops, steaks, liver and sausages and for patties made from prepared minced meat. The meat is placed in hot fat in the frying pan and fried to a golden brown on both sides.

GRILLING. This is a quick way of cooking meat, usually chops and steaks. The grill must be red hot and the grid greased. Place meat on grid until one side is nicely browned, turn and cook on other side. Turn once only.

ROASTING. The most suitable cut of meat for this method of cooking is Rib or Prime Bola or a Corner Cut of Prime Bola in red meat, and the shoulder of veal or lamb where white meat is desired.

Place the seasoned meat on a grid in a baking dish containing a little water and fat. Place the dish in a pre-heated oven for 15 minutes to seal the juices. Lower the temperature of the oven somewhat and baste the meat once or twice during cooking.

STEWING. Use the cheaper cuts of meat as this method of long and slow cooking will tenderise tough meat. Cut meat into serving pieces and brown in a little fat in a saucepan. Barely cover with boiling water of stock, bring to the boil, season and reduce heat so that the meat simmers only. Peeled and cut up onions and carrots are usually added.

TIMES OF COOKING FOR BAKING AND ROASTING

Beef   Allow 15 minutes to the pound and 15 minutes over (Less or more according to desired 'rareness').
Veal   Allow 25 minutes to the pound.
Lamb Allow 20 minutes to the pound and 20 minutes over.

ROAST SHOULDER OF LAMB

1 shoulder of lamb   a few mint leaves
seasoning

The meat may be boned or cooked on the bone as desired. Tuck the mint leaves into the meat, season. Place in an oven dish in a pre-heated oven and proceed as for roasting.

Serve with roast potatoes, or boiled new potatoes, green peas and mint sauce.

LAMB CHOPS

4 chops (the best chops are those from the neck end)

Lamb chops are best grilled, and served with chipped potatoes or boiled new potatoes, green peas and mint sauce. They should definitely not be overcooked.

Proceed as instructions for grilling (see page 66).

ROAST BREAST OF LAMB

1 breast of lamb   1 small onion
seasoning   few mint leaves

Place meat in oven dish, tuck mint leaves in and place the peeled and grated onion over the top. Add a little seasoning and proceed as directed for roasting (see page 66).

Serve with mint sauce and desired vegetables.

VEAL

Veal takes longer to cook than lamb and must be well cooked. Choose veal that is very pale in colour.

ROAST VEAL

The shoulder and breast are best for roasting, and are generally stuffed. Cooking time 40 minutes per pound. Substitute paprika pepper for ordinary pepper when cooking veal.

ROAST VEAL

The shoulder is generally used for roasting and can be cooked on the bone or boned. If the latter, it is nicer stuffed.

1 shoulder of veal	seasoning
1 large onion	3 tablespoons chicken fat

Season meat and place peeled and thinly sliced onion on top. Spread fat all over. Put in pre-heated oven and proceed as for roasting. If the meat is cooked in tinfoil it will be juicy and more tender.

ROAST STUFFED VEAL

1 shoulder or breast of veal	Dumpling stuffing (see page 90)
seasoning	3 tablespoons chicken fat

Have the butcher bone the meat. If the breast is being used, then have a pocket made and put stuffing into it. For the shoulder spread the stuffing over the meat. Season, put fat over, roll and tie securely, and roast as directed for roasting (see page 66). This dish is improved when wrapped in tinfoil before roasting.

VEAL CHOPS

4 veal chops   paprika pepper
fat for frying

Dust chops with paprika and place in hot fat in a frying pan. They should be cooked rather slowly, until browned on both sides.

VEAL SOUFFLÉ

8 oz. minced veal $1\frac{1}{2}$ oz. flour
$\frac{1}{2}$ pint stock $1\frac{1}{2}$ oz. fat
3 eggs   seasoning and a little
     paprika pepper

Make a roux with the fat and flour in a saucepan. Add liquid and bring to boil, add meat. Remove pan from heat, add well beaten egg yolks and season well. Return pan to heat and cook for a minute and stir until mixture thickens. Fold in very gently the well whisked egg whites and transfer mixture to a greased oval oven dish so that it is two thirds full. Place the dish in a pan of cold water and bake in a preheated moderate oven for 40 minutes. Turn out and serve *immediately* with desired vegetables. On NO account open the oven during cooking time as this would cause the soufflé to sink.

BRAISED BREAST OF VEAL

1 breast of veal   stuffing (see page 90 for
seasoning   Dumpling Stuffing)
     lemon juice

Have the butcher bone meat and make a pocket right down the breast. (Save bones for making stock.) Season with salt, pepper and lemon juice, fill with the stuffing, roll and tie securely. Proceed as directions for braising (see page 66).

VEAL AND EGG PIE

1½ lb. minced veal
2 small onions
1 carrot
some veal bones
3 eggs

1 pint water for stock
1 teaspoon tomato purée
seasoning
4 oz. short pastry

Make stock with bones, carrot and 1 onion. Mix the veal with tomato purée and the other onion peeled and minced. Season well, and place in greased deep oblong oven dish. Scoop out three hollows along the top of meat, making sure the bottom of the dish is still covered with meat. Break an egg into each circle, being very careful not to break yolks. Add a little stock to dish, and cover with pastry rolled out ¼ inch thick, making two or three slits to allow steam to escape. Bake in a pre-heated moderately hot oven for 15 minutes, lower heat and cook for further 45 minutes. If this dish is to be served cold, when the pie is absolutely cooled pour the remaining cooled stock through a small funnel into the pie through slits in the pastry. Leave overnight, and the stock will have jellied.

WIENER SCHNITZEL

4 very thin slices of veal
1 oz. flour seasoned with
  salt and pepper
little paprika pepper

1 egg
chicken fat for frying
breadcrumbs
wedges of lemon

Dust meat with paprika pepper and dip into seasoned flour, then into beaten egg and white breadcrumbs. Heat fat in a frying pan and fry meat until golden brown and crisp on both sides. Serve on hot dish with wedges of lemon and a few stoned olives.

CHOPMEAT

1½ lb. chuck steak	2 tablespoons medium matzo
1 onion	meal or breadcrumbs
2 eggs	seasoning

Mince meat and onion. Add meal or breadcrumbs, lightly beaten eggs and seasoning.

Form into patties and fry in hot fat until browned on one side, turn and fry on the other side or bake in the oven.

These are extra nice served with fried onions and mashed potatoes and at a meal where Borshcht is the soup course.

CHOPMEAT AND RICE WITH TOMATO SAUCE
(6 Servings)

1½ lb. meat	8 oz. rice
¼ bay leaf	1 teaspoon paprika

Mince the meat as in recipe for chopmeat (see page 71), but add ¼ bay leaf crushed and 1 small teaspoon paprika. Form into medium sized balls and cook in the following sauce for 1 hour.

TOMATO SAUCE

1 large onion	6 drops each of Worcester-
1 medium sized tin tomatoes	shire and tomato sauces
fat	

Cut up onion very small and brown lightly in a little fat. Place all ingredients in a saucepan with a little water and boil gently for several minutes. Add the meat which should be barely covered with liquid. Cover pan tightly and boil gently for 1 hour.

While meat is cooking, boil rice and keep very hot. Place portion of rice on each plate and add 2 or 3 meat balls with some of the sauce.

BAKED CHOPMEAT

1½ lb. chuck steak prepared   ½ pint stock
    as *Chopmeat* (see page 71)   seasonings

Place the prepared meat in a greased oven dish. Add stock
and bake in a fairly hot oven for 1 hour.

BRAISED BEEF

2 lb. short rib   1 onion
seasoning   1 carrot
2 oz. fat   3 sticks celery

Melt the fat in a saucepan and brown the meat on all sides.
Add vegetables peeled and cut up and brown these also. Add
just enough water or stock to hardly cover meat, season, bring
to the boil and simmer for 2 hours. Two or three peeled
tomatoes can be added if desired to improve flavour.

HAMBURGERS IN TOMATO SAUCE

1½ lb. chuck steak prepared   ½ pint tomato juice
    as *Chopmeat* (see page 71)   ½ pint stock
fat for frying   seasoning to taste

Shape the prepared meat into small patties and fry gently for
a minute on both sides. Bring the tomato juice and stock to
the boil in a saucepan, carefully lower the patties into the
liquid, season, cover the saucepan tightly and simmer for
30 minutes. If desired the liquid can be thickened with a little
flour.

SALT BEEF

3 lb. pickled beef	3 bay leaves
water	6 peppercorns
1 onion	1 carrot

Place the meat in a saucepan and cover with cold water. Bring to the boil quickly and then discard the water. Cover the meat again with cold water, bring to the boil, skim, add all other ingredients and boil gently for at least 2½ hours or until tender. Cold salt beef, sliced thinly, makes very good sandwiches.

CHOLENT

This is the traditional Jewish dish served for lunch on the Sabbath day in orthodox homes when no cooking is done on that day. It is prepared on the Friday and cooked in a large casserole or dish with a very tight fitting lid. The cholent is put in a very slow oven just before the Sabbath commences (at sundown on Friday) and left until the next day.

I do not think this dish is so universally used as in former years, but it is still a favourite and an appetising dish.

1½ lb. rather fat meat	1 small onion
4 oz. haricot beans	1 small carrot
4 oz. medium barley	seasoning
6 medium sized potatoes	dumplings (see page 90)

Put the meat at the bottom of the dish and surround it with beans, barley, finely cut up onion and carrot, and then the peeled potatoes (left whole). Make small dumplings and place these on top. Season well, fill the dish with boiling water, cover tightly and bake in a very slow oven.

GOULASH

1½ lb. stewing steak
1½ pints water
½ pint tomato juice
2 or 3 tomatoes
2 small onions

1 glass white wine (optional)
1 oz. flour
2 oz. fat or margarine
clove garlic (optional)
seasoning

Cut meat into small serving pieces and fry in a saucepan over gentle heat in 1 oz. fat until nicely browned. Add stock, tomato juice, peeled tomatoes, wine and seasoning. Bring to the boil and simmer gently until meat is tender (1¼ hours). In another pan make a roux with the remainder of fat and flour and strain liquid from other pan on to this. Bring to the boil, stirring well, simmer gently for 5 minutes, adjust seasoning, add meat and vegetables and a dash of paprika. Serve very hot.

I like to serve this goulash on a bed of hot plain boiled long grained rice. This may not be recommended by conservative cooks, but it is extra good, all the same.

STEAK AND MUSHROOM PUDDING

1½ lb. stewing steak
2 onions
4 oz. mushrooms

seasoning
water or stock
8 oz. suet pastry (see page 115)

Cut meat into 1-inch squares. Roll out pastry ¼ inch thick and cut off a piece large enough to cover top of basin. With remaining pastry, line a 2-pint pudding basin and place the seasoned meat, onions, and mushrooms in alternate layers to 1 inch from top of basin. Fill it three quarters full of stock, cover with remaining pastry, making sure edges are sealed. Cover and tie with a floured pudding cloth and boil for 2½ hours or steam for 3½ hours. Serve with hot gravy.

POT ROAST WITH MUSHROOMS AND GREEN PEPPER

1½ lb. chuck steak
1 small tin tomatoes
1 onion
1 carrot
2 tablespoon fat

1 small green pepper
4 oz. mushrooms
seasoning
½ glass water

Melt fat in a saucepan and when hot put in meat and brown well on all sides. Add tomatoes and seasoning. Bring to the boil, and cook gently until meat is tender, about 2 hours. Add the onion, carrot, pepper, and mushrooms, all sliced, an hour before end of cooking time.

Serve with boiled or mashed potatoes and some of the gravy.

POT ROAST

1½ lb. meat (chuck steak
    is very suitable)
2 tablespoons fat
1 onion

2 cups water or stock
2 or 3 tomatoes
vegetables
seasoning

Melt fat in a saucepan and when hot put in meat and brown well on all sides. Add onion peeled and cut up, water, tomatoes and seasonings. The meat must simmer only, and will take about 2 hours. Finally cut up potatoes and carrots may be added an hour before end of cooking time.

CHILI CON CARNE

1½ lb. stewing steak   1 small onion
2 tablespoon fat   ½ teaspoon salt
1 clove garlic   3 or 4 teaspoons
                           chili powder

Cut meat into very small pieces and brown well in heated fat in saucepan. Mince garlic and onion and add, then add salt and chili powder. The amount of chili powder will depend solely on the individual taste and should be added carefully. Simmer very gently, adding water as needed, for about 2 hours. Serve hot with beans and crisp bread.

BEEF OLIVES

1½ lb. steak   1 oz. flour
1 small onion   ¼ pint stock or water
1 oz. fat   seasoning

Have the butcher cut steak into very thin slices and then cut these into pieces about 4 inches by 3 inches. Spread a little of the dressing on each piece, roll up and secure well with fine white string. Melt fat in a saucepan and when hot brown the olives well on all sides. Remove from pan and put in the sliced onion and fry for a few minutes. Sprinkle in flour, stock and seasoning and stir until boiling. Replace the meat olives, cover pan tightly and cook gently for 1½ hours.

Serve on a bed of hot mashed potato and pour the gravy around.

CORNISH PASTIES

12 oz. chuck steak	1 large onion
1 large potato	1 tablespoon stock
seasoning	12 oz. short pastry
1 egg white	

Peel and parboil potato and dice. Mince meat and onion separately. Season meat and moisten with the stock. Roll out pastry thinly and cut into $3\frac{1}{2}$-inch squares. Place some meat, then onion and potato in each square, leaving a $\frac{1}{4}$-inch margin all round. Fold pastry over, making sure edges are absolutely sealed. Brush over with a little beaten white of egg, make small slit in centre of pasties to allow steam to escape and bake in a moderately hot oven for 20 minutes. Lower heat and cook for a further 25 minutes.

MEAT STEW

$1\frac{1}{2}$ lb. stewing steak	2 oz. medium barley
2 onions	2 oz. haricot beans
2 carrots	2 pints water or stock
6 medium sized potatoes	seasoning

Peel vegetables and place with all other ingredients in a large saucepan. Cover with boiling water, season, and simmer for $2\frac{1}{2}$ hours. This is equally successful cooked in a moderately slow oven in a casserole. Make sure the saucepan or casserole is tightly covered.

IRISH STEW

2 lb. scrag of lamb
  or mutton
2 large onions
1 large carrot
seasoning

3 sticks celery
2 tablespoons medium
  barley
1½ lb. potatoes (small)
water

Cut meat into serving pieces and place in a saucepan. Add peeled and cut up onions, carrots, celery and barley. Add the peeled potatoes, season and add water to barely cover. Put lid on saucepan and simmer for 2½ hours.

OXTAIL

1 oxtail (jointed)
2 onions
2 carrots
1 glass sherry

1½ pints water or stock
1 oz. flour
1 oz. fat
seasoning

Melt fat in a saucepan and brown the joints of the oxtail. Add peeled and cut up vegetables, sherry, stock or water and seasoning. Bring to the boil and boil gently for 3 hours. Thicken the liquid with the flour, readjust seasoning and serve very hot with desired vegetables.

CURRIES

In the olden days, Jewish cookery never included curries, but no modern cookery book would be complete without at least a few words on this subject. Apart from curry dishes being popular, left-over meats, fish and vegetables can be used to make very tasty dishes.

The different 'left-overs' to be served should be cut up, and simmered very slowly in the sauce for about 15 minutes so that the flavour can be well imparted to the ingredients.

Curries are usually served on a bed of plain boiled rice. If desired, chutney can be handed round separately.

A recipe for curry sauce will be found on page 108.

CURRIED BEEF

1½ lb. stewing steak	2 carrots
1 oz. flour	1 teaspoon curry powder
1 oz. fat	(or to taste)
2 onions	¼ pint tomato juice
1 pint stock	2 oz. seeded raisins
	seasoning

Melt fat in a saucepan. Add flour and curry powder and cook gently for 2 minutes, mixing well. Stir in tomato juice and stock and bring to the boil. Put in meat cut into small pieces, peeled cut onion, sliced carrots, raisins and seasoning. Cover the pan tightly and simmer for 2 hours. Serve on a bed of plain hot boiled rice.

CURRIED VEAL

1½ lb. stewing veal	1 teaspoon curry powder
1 oz. flour	(or to taste)
1 oz. fat	¼ pint tomato juice
2 onions	2 oz. seeded raisins
2 carrots	seasoning

The method of cooking is similar to that for *Curried Beef*.

HEARTS

The very small calves' hearts are best, and the nicest way of cooking is stuffing and then roasting or braising them. The butcher will remove all veins and make a pocket for stuffing (see page 90 for Dumpling stuffing).

TONGUE

1 tongue (this will be pickled by the butcher)

The method of cooking is the same as for *Salt Beef* (see p. 73) but cooking time will be 3 hours.
To skin. Place the hot cooked tongue on a board and quickly peel off the skin from the tip downwards.
To press. Form the hot peeled tongue into a circle and place it in a basin with a plate *on top of the tongue*. Put some heavy weights on the plate and leave overnight if possible.

LIVER

1 lb. calf's liver	fat for frying
or tender ox liver	2 onions
½ pint stock or water	seasoning
1 tablespoon flour	

Peel and slice onions and fry in fat. Remove from pan and keep hot. Cut the liver into fairly thin slices season and fry in the same fat until browned on each side. Take from pan and keep hot with the onions. Mix the flour and stock together and when smooth, pour into fat in pan and stir until thickened. Return the onions to the pan and serve this gravy with the liver and desired vegetables.

POULTRY AND STUFFINGS

The poulterer will pluck, singe and draw the birds or cut them up into desired portions. It is now possible to buy frozen poultry ready for cooking. This saves a remarkable amount of work.

For soup making, a boiling hen or a pullet is used and this may be baked afterwards. All fat is removed from poultry, rendered down and used for cooking purposes.

Poultry is kashered in the same way as meat, but before cooking it is scalded with boiling water and the skin scraped thoroughly.

TIMES FOR ROASTING POULTRY

	Oven temperature	Time per pound
Capon or Roasting Chicken	Moderate	30 minutes
Duck	Very moderate	20—30 minutes
Duckling	Moderate	20—25 minutes
Goose	Very moderate	25 minutes
Turkey - small	Moderate	20 minutes
Turkey - large	Very moderate	15—20 minutes

BOILED CHICKEN

1 boiling fowl	½ lemon
2 onions	seasoning
water	Béchamel sauce with egg
2 carrots	(see page 105)

Prepare the fowl and rub breast with the lemon. Place in saucepan with just enough water to cover; bring to the boil, skim, add peeled vegetables, seasoning and boil gently for about 3 hours, or until tender. Serve with sauce and desired vegetables.

ROAST CHICKEN

1 capon or roaster	1 wedge lemon
seasoning	

Season the prepared chicken and rub the inside with lemon. Completely wrap the bird in tinfoil or in greased grease-proof paper. Place in baking dish into which one cup of seasoned boiling water has been added. Bake in a preheated moderately hot oven for about 2½ hours, removing the wrapping for the last 15 minutes of cooking time to ensure crispness.

STUFFED ROAST CHICKEN

Proceed as for *Roast Chicken*, with either *Chopmeat* or *Dumpling* Stuffing (pages 71, 90). If using dumpling, do not pack too tightly to allow stuffing to expand.

CHICKEN CASSEROLE

1 boiling fowl (cut into
  serving pieces)
3 onions
2 carrots
2 oz. fat
1½ pints stock

1 clove garlic
4 oz. mushrooms
1 celery heart
1 glass sherry
seasoning

Heat fat and fry fowl until brown on both sides then transfer to a casserole. Add stock, peeled and sliced vegetables and all other ingredients. Cover tightly and cook in slow oven for 3½ hours, or until fowl is tender. The liquid can be thickened with a beaten egg yolk or a little flour.

CHICKEN PIE

1 cooked boiling fowl
½ teaspoon mixed herbs

8 oz. short or flaky pastry
  (see page 114)
½ pint stock

Cut flesh from fowl into strips and place in a large pie dish. Pour over stock and sprinkle herbs on top. Cover with rolled-out pastry, making 2 or 3 slits for steam to escape. Place in hot oven for 15 minutes and then bake further for 25 minutes in a moderate oven.

CHICKEN PILAFF

1 boiling fowl	4 oz. rice
pint stock	1 oz. fat
seasoning	Béchamel sauce with egg
2½ pints water	(see page 105)

Boil prepared fowl as directed in water and seasoning. When tender lift out carefully, draining well, and place on a dish. In large frying pan melt fat, add rice and fry for 4 minutes. Add 1 pint boiling stock, cover pan and cook very gently until all liquid is absorbed (about 25 minutes). Meanwhile remove all flesh from fowl, cut into small pieces, and add to rice during last 10 minutes of cooking time. Serve pilaff with sauce and garnish with cooked mushrooms if desired.

CHICKEN TIMBALE

1 lb. cooked minced chicken	seasoning
1 pint veal stock	2 oz. mushrooms
2 egg yolks	

Grill mushrooms and place in the bottom of a greased baking dish. Beat egg yolks into the stock, add minced chicken, season to taste and pour over the mushrooms in the dish. Place dish in another baking dish with cold water coming half-way up the sides and bake in a moderate oven for 50 minutes or until set firmly. Leave until cold.

If preferred, this mixture can be baked in 4 small individual baking dishes.

CHICKEN CROQUETTES

See *Croquettes*, page 100.

CHICKEN RISSOLES

12 oz. cooked, minced chicken   1 onion
3 eggs   breadcrumbs
seasoning   fat for frying

Mince peeled onion and the chicken, add seasoning and 2 eggs.
Add enough breadcrumbs to bind mixture, and with floured
hands shape into flat, round patties. Coat with remaining egg,
beaten, and dip into breadcrumbs, making sure the patties are
completely coated. Let them stand in a cool place for 1 hour
and then fry slowly in hot shallow fat on both sides.

CHICKEN MARYLAND

1 very young capon   fat for frying
1 egg   seasoning
dried breadcrumbs

The chicken should be cut into serving pieces, and seasoned.
Dip the chicken pieces into beaten egg and then into breadcrumbs until well coated. Leave for 1 hour. Brown the chicken
pieces in plenty of hot fat rather quickly and then cook slowly
for 35 minutes, turning occasionally. Serve with corn fritters
(see page 98).

CHICKEN VOL-AU-VENT

12 oz. puff pastry (see page 116)   1½ cups stock
12 oz. cooked minced chicken   4 oz. cooked minced
little cornflour   mushrooms
seasoning

Make 1 large or 4 individual vol-au-vent cases. Thicken
stock with cornflour, add seasoning, mushrooms and chicken.
Heap some of the mixture into the baked vol-au-vent cases
and reheat in a very hot oven for 4 or 5 minutes.

ROAST DUCK OR DUCKLING

Duck is stuffed and roasted like chicken, but omit lemon and rub with a cut clove of garlic instead.

ROAST DUCKLING WITH APPLES AND PRUNES

1 duckling apple and prune stuffing
seasoning   (see page 89)

Pack the stuffing loosely into the duckling, pepper and salt well, wrap in tinfoil or greaseproof paper and cook as directed. Remove paper during last 15 minutes of cooking time and baste with the heated liquid in which the prunes were cooked.
 Serve with green peas, boiled potatoes and a tablespoon of hot juice.

DUCK WITH ORANGE

1 duckling   little sugar
4 oranges   ½ pint stock
1 liqueur glass cointreau ½ pint orange juice
margarine   little cornflour

Bake duck as directed (see top of page), but place 3 or 4 slices of orange on breast of bird, basting frequently with mixture of stock and orange juice. Meanwhile, skin, seed and cut oranges into thinnish slices, and fry in a little hot margarine. Sprinkle with castor sugar and drain. From the baking dish drain liquid, skim off all fat, then thicken with cornflour. Place in a saucepan (keeping the duck hot meanwhile) and cook very gently for 2 minutes, add cointreau and stir well. Serve the duck with one or two orange slices and hand round sauce. Serve with green peas and another vegetable if desired.

DUCK WITH PINEAPPLE

1 duckling
¼ pint sweetened
   pineapple juice
1 glass sherry

1 medium sized tin
   pineapple chunks
½ pint stock

Prepare and roast duck as directed (see page 86). Baste with mixture of stock and juice, and add sherry instead of cointreau when making the sauce. Heat the pineapple cubes in the syrup from the tin and serve with the duck.

ROAST GOOSE

This is a bird which has an excess of fat and for this reason is not so popular as duckling or turkey.

The best way is to roast it in a pre-heated moderate oven for about 1 hour and then pour off the fat which has run from the bird. Cool goose. When cold, stuff with desired filling, season with little salt, pepper, crushed clove of garlic and ½ teaspoon of ground ginger. Now cook as directed for chicken or duck.

Serve with apple sauce.

TURKEY

Two stuffings are generally used for turkeys and I list below a few suggestions:

Sausage meat and Chestnut stuffing
Apple and potato and Veal forcemeat
Dumpling stuffing and sage and onion stuffing
Prepared chopmeat and dumpling stuffing.

Left-over turkey can be used for croquettes, salads and sandwiches or sliced and re-heated in gravy.

For seasoning, use a little salt, pepper and ground ginger.

STUFFINGS

A good stuffing is very much like a good sauce. Its use is to improve the flavour of the food with which it is served. It must never be stodgy and should never be packed too tightly as this leads to sogginess.

Stuffing may also be used to reduce the richness of duck, for instance, in which case orange is recommended.

CHESTNUT STUFFING

1 lb. chestnuts
stock
1 small onion, finely chopped

seasoning
2 oz. melted margarine
  or chicken fat
breadcrumbs

Make a gash in each chestnut, place in cold water, bring to boil and boil for 5 minutes. Drain and remove shells and skins and put through a sieve. Add all other ingredients and enough breadcrumbs to make a fairly stiff mixture.

CELERY STUFFING

1 large head of celery
8 oz. breadcrumbs
1 tablespoon lemon juice
2 beaten eggs

1 oz. margarine or fat
1 grated onion
seasoning

Cook well-washed celery in a little salted water until tender, then chop very finely. Add all other ingredients and enough breadcrumbs to make a firm mixture.

APPLE AND POTATO STUFFING

1 lb. cooking apples
2 onions
1 gill orange juice

little seasoning
4 boiled potatoes
½ teaspoon mixed herbs

Peel and chop apples and onions finely. Put in saucepan, add a little seasoning, herbs, juice and simmer until cooked. Press through a sieve and add enough mashed potato to make a firm mixture.

SAUSAGE MEAT STUFFING

1 lb. sausage meat
1 onion, peeled and minced
1 oz. melted margarine
1 egg, beaten lightly

seasoning
breadcrumbs
½ teaspoon mixed herbs

Mix all ingredients well together to form a fairly firm mixture.

APPLE AND PRUNE STUFFING

12 large prunes
3 large cooking apples
2 oz. chopped walnuts
sugar

lemon wedge
2 oz. melted margarine
1 egg, beaten
breadcrumbs

Cook prunes in sweetened water with a wedge of lemon until tender. Remove stones and chop. Add apples, peeled, cored and chopped very finely, nuts, margarine, beaten egg, a little seasoning and sufficient breadcrumbs to bind.

MINCED VEAL STUFFING

8 oz. veal   1 onion
2 oz. mushrooms   1 oz. melted margarine
breadcrumbs or matzo meal   seasoning
1 beaten egg

Put veal, mushrooms and peeled onion through mincer. Add seasoning, beaten egg, fat, and enough breadcrumbs or matzo meal to bind. This is very good for stuffing a chicken or one end of a turkey.

SAGE AND ONION STUFFING

1 lb. onions   seasoning
4 oz. breadcrumbs   ½ teaspoon dried sage

Peel and boil onions until tender, then chop them very finely. Mix with other ingredients and season.

DUMPLINGS

4 oz. flour   salt and pepper
1½ oz. margarine   cold water

Mix ingredients, add just enough cold water to make the consistency not too thick.
(As Stuffing) This dumpling mixture is also used by Jewish cooks as a stuffing for hearts, roast or braised breast of veal, or roast chicken. In order to make the consistency looser than for ordinary dumplings, the mixture is often bound with an egg. When stuffing a chicken, care should be taken not to use too much, in order to allow room for expansion.

EGG DISHES

Of all the many varieties of food, there is probably no single item richer in nourishment or more useful to the housewife than the humble egg. Indispensable for baking or in the preparation of sauces, puddings and custards and batters, it is also capable of endless variations when served in its own right. And since the egg contains protein, essential minerals and vitamins, it should be remembered that it is also an excellent substitute for meat.

Each housewife will develop her own favourite methods and recipes for the preparation of eggs, whether she chooses to serve them as a tasty snack, such as Scotch eggs, or as an omlette for a delicious and satisfying main course. But in whatever form they come to the table, eggs should be considered an essential part of the family's daily diet.

CURRIED EGGS

1 Serving

1 egg	a few sultanas
2 oz. cooked rice	curry sauce (see page 108)

Poach or hard boil the egg as desired and place on a small mound of hot cooked rice to which has been added a few sultanas. Pour the curry sauce over the egg.

POACHED EGGS

Eggs are more successfully poached in a frying pan. Slip each egg into boiling water to which has been added a little salt and a teaspoon of brown vinegar.

Spoon some of the liquid over the yolk to cover it and cook gently for 3 minutes. Lift out carefully with a slice and serve on hot buttered toast, a bed of spinach, or a mound of hot mashed potatoes.

SCRAMBLED EGGS

1 Serving

2 eggs	4 tablespoons milk or water
large knob of butter	salt

Beat the eggs well, add the milk or water and a large pinch of salt. Melt the fat in a saucepan and when just turning a very light brown, pour in the egg, stirring continuously. Scrambled eggs should be creamy and not set firm.

SOUFFLÉS

See pages 140, 141, 142

OMELETTE

1 Serving

Many people consider that eggs for an omelette should only be beaten very slightly, just enough to mix yolk and white; others like the yolks beaten separately, then folded into the stiffly beaten egg whites, but I find that my recipe produces a very good fluffy omelette.

Fillings for plain omelettes can be varied to make delicious luncheon or supper dishes, or different flavouring ingredients may be added to mixture before cooking.

2 eggs	1 tablespoon cold water or milk
½ oz. butter	salt

Beat the eggs well with the milk or water and add a large pinch of salt. Melt the butter in an omelette pan and when hot (but not discoloured) pour in the mixture. Cook over gentle heat until lightly set, loosen the sides with a knife to allow all the uncooked mixture to run underneath. When the bottom of the omelette is lightly browned, and all the uncooked mixture has run underneath, fold the omelette over in half in the pan, slip on to a hot plate and *serve immediately*.

SOME FILLINGS FOR OMELETTES

CHEESE: Add 1 tablespoon grated cheese to the egg mixture.
CREAM CHEESE: Mix 2 oz. cream cheese with 1 dessertspoon granulated sugar. Spread this on top of omelette during the cooking and before folding over.
MUSHROOM: Fry 4 or 5 chopped mushrooms in a separate pan and place on omelette before folding over.
TOMATO: Fry 2 peeled tomatoes cut into thick slices and place on omelette before folding over.
JAM: Spread 1 dessertspoon warmed jam on omelette before folding over. This omelette can be served as a sweet.

EGGS MORNAY

1 Serving

1 egg   little grated cheese
portion of hot mashed potato   Mornay sauce (see page 105)

Poach the egg and place it on a mound of hot mashed potato which has been mixed with a little grated cheese. Pour cheese sauce over egg.

SCOTCH EGGS

4 hard-boiled eggs   breadcrumbs
1 raw egg   fat for frying
6 oz. raw sausage meat

Shell the hard-boiled eggs and cover them with the meat, taking care that they are completely coated. Egg and bread-crumb them and fry until golden brown. Cut in half length-wise and serve hot with any desired vegetables, or they can be eaten cold with a salad.

EGG SOUBISE

1 Serving

1 egg   1 oz. butter or margarine
portion of hot mashed potato   Soubise sauce (see page 105)
1 small onion

Peel and fry the finely cut up onion in the fat and mix with the potatoes. Poach the egg and place on top of the potato mixture and pour the onion sauce over the egg.

BLINTZES, PANCAKES AND FRITTERS

Blintzes are essentially a stuffed pancake, the usual fillings being either cream cheese or minced meat, the former being one of the traditional dishes served at the Festival of Pentecost.

Pancakes can be made into a very delectable sweet by the addition of recommended fillings, such as cooked and sieved apple, jam, cream cheese mixed with chopped nuts or with chopped apple.

BLINTZES

1 egg	1 cup flour
½ teaspoon salt	1 cup water
cooking oil	

Beat egg slightly with salt and water. Stir in flour and make a very smooth batter. Heat frying pan and grease it (using oil). Pour in 2 tablespoons of batter, tilting pan so that the bottom is covered. Cook over gentle heat on one side only until just set, but not brown. Turn out on to clean cloth, cooked side uppermost and repeat with remainder of the batter. Place 1 large tablespoon of filling on cooked side of each blintze, fold over, press edges well together and fry on both sides until golden brown.

MEAT BLINTZES

6 oz. left-over cooked meat	2 tablespoon stock or
seasoning	tomato ketchup
1 small onion	1 egg

Mince meat and onion, add seasoning, stock or ketchup, bind with beaten egg, and mix well. Proceed as for *Blintzes* and serve with gravy or tomato sauce.

APPLE BLINTZES

8 oz. cooking apples	1 oz. sugar
1 oz. ground almonds	cinnamon to taste
grated rind of 1 lemon	

Grate the peeled apples and mix with other ingredients. Proceed as for *Blintzes*. When cooked, sprinkle with sugar and cinnamon.

CHEESE BLINTZES

8 oz. cream cheese   sugar
1 egg   little grated
seasoning   lemon rind

Add beaten egg, little salt and pepper, lemon rind and sugar to taste to the cheese. Mix well and proceed as for *Blintzes*. A little sour cream may be served with this dish.

This dish is generally served at Shavuoth (the Festival of Pentecost).

SIMPLE PANCAKE BATTER

4 oz. plain flour   pinch salt
½ pint milk or water   1 egg

Place sieved flour and salt in bowl. Make well in the centre and break egg into it and add half the liquid. With wooden spoon, and starting from the centre, stir clockwise gradually bringing in flour from the outside edge. Add remainder of liquid slowly and mix thoroughly until batter is perfectly smooth. Whenever possible, allow mixture to stand for 1 hour in a cold place before using.

Heat ½ oz. fat in thick frying pan and when hot pour off excess fat. Pour in just enough batter to cover bottom of pan thinly and cook over medium heat until set. Turn pancake carefully and cook other side until slightly brown. Serve folded on hot dish with lemon juice and sugar or jam as desired.

FRITTERS

Batter: 4 oz. plain flour   pinch salt
½ oz. sugar   1 egg
¼ pint milk or water

Make batter as for pancakes, but the mixture will be much thicker owing to only half the amount of liquid used.

It is a matter of choice what fruit is used, but the most popular are:

Apples — Peel and core sweet apples and cut into ¼-inch rings.

Banana — Peel bananas and cut lengthwise.

Pineapple — Tinned rings of pineapple, well drained.

To cook fritters. Place fruit in batter, leave for a minute, lift out carefully and fry in very hot fat on both sides until golden brown. Do not cook too many fritters in pan at the same time.

CORN FRITTERS

1 tin sweet corn   seasoning
2 eggs   fat for frying
breadcrumbs

Beat eggs until frothy, add corn, seasoning and enough bread-crumbs to bind mixture. Shape into flat patties and fry gently in shallow fat until golden brown. These are served with Chicken Maryland (see page 85).

CROQUETTES, RISSOLES AND RICE DISHES

These are good ways of using up any left-over meat or fish. The dish can be used as an entrée or can be served as the main course. The difference between croquettes and rissoles is that the mixture for croquettes is encased in egg and breadcrumbs and fried, whereas for rissoles the mixture is encased in a thin pastry case and fried in fat or oil. The process for both is the same, i. e. a thick binding sauce mixed with either the minced or finely chopped meat or fish. A little experimenting may be necessary to determine the exact amount of sauce to use to produce the desired consistency. As explained earlier, milk can only be used for fish croquettes and stock for meat croquettes.

CHICKEN CROQUETTES

12 oz. chopped cold chicken   binding sauce
4 oz. cooked chopped mushrooms   (see page 104)
little chopped onion   2 eggs
fat   some breadcrumbs

Mix the cold ingredients with boiling hot binding sauce and when cool add 1 egg beaten well and mix thoroughly. Spread out evenly $\frac{1}{2}$ inch thick on a plate and leave until absolutely cold. Shape into portions about 3 inches by 1 inch, dip in egg and breadcrumbs and fry in deep fat until golden brown. Serve with mushroom sauce.

FISH CROQUETTES

Use 10 oz. flaked cooked haddock (this fish is the best for making croquettes) and the procedure is the same. Oil should be used for the frying.

Serve with tomato or tartare sauce (pages 109, 110) with wedges of lemon.

EGG CROQUETTES
(hard-boiled eggs)

The eggs should be chopped into small pieces, then proceed as for fish croquettes. Serve with tartare sauce (see page 110).

RISSOLES

The basic mixtures are exactly the same as used for the croquettes, but instead of coating with egg and breadcrumbs, roll out very thinly a sheet of short pastry (see page 114). Cut this into squares of 4 inches and place 1 tablespoon of the desired mixture into the centre. Fold over, making sure the edges are well sealed. Fry in deep fat until golden brown.

RISOTTO

4 oz. rice	1 oz. butter or margarine
1½ pints water or stock	salt
½ pint tomato juice	a little paprika pepper
3 oz. grated cheese	

Wash and drain the rice and sauté it in the butter or margarine. Add tomato juice, stock and seasoning. Cover the saucepan tightly and cook gently until all liquid has been absorbed. Work in the grated cheese with a fork.

By adding extra ingredients, risotto may become a very satisfying dish and I list a few suggestions below:
1. Fry mushrooms and peas with the rice.
2. Diced chicken or any cooked diced meat fried with the rice, but of course omitting the cheese.
3. Fry some cold flaked white fish with the rice.

CHEESE RICE

4 oz. rice	1 small tin tomato purée
2 oz. cheese	seasoning
breadcrumbs	1 oz. butter or margarine

Boil and drain the rice. Add the tomato purée, grated cheese and seasoning. Put into a greased oven dish, cover with breadcrumbs, dot with butter or margarine and bake in a hot oven until nicely browned.

SAVOURY AND SWEET SAUCES

The most ordinary dish can be made into a party dish by the addition of a good sauce, and the originality of the cook here comes into play. On the other hand, the most appetizing dish can be ruined by a bad or wrong sauce.

The most common fault is that the sauce is lumpy, tasteless or out of keeping with the dish with which it is served. There is no excuse for a lumpy sauce as this is only the result of not giving enough attention to detail.

The reason for a tasteless sauce is obvious, and one must be careful to make sure the sauce has a bearing on the dish with which it is served.

SAVOURY SAUCES

TO MAKE SAUCES

The basis of most sauces is the liquid (stock) thickened by a roux (fat and flour), or by egg yolks, or by long slow cooking to reduce the liquid to the desired consistency. The outstanding factor here is the stock and the right amount of seasoning.

Consistency of a sauce is important. It should be remembered that the sauce should never be too thin, as this would result in the dish 'swimming' in it, or too thick so that it could not be poured freely. The approximate quantities for sauces are as follows:

Pouring sauce: 1 oz. fat
      1 oz. flour to ¾ pint liquid
Thick binding sauce (as used in croquettes and rissoles):
      1 oz. fat
      1 oz. flour
      ¼ pint liquid

The two main sauces are béchamel sauce and velouté sauce. Béchamel sauce is made with milk and velouté sauce is made with meat stock.

For the cook who has ample time, when using milk for savoury sauces, the flavour will be greatly enhanced if the milk is prepared in the following way:

Dice one small onion and two small carrots, one small leek and fry gently in butter slowly, add 1 pint milk, 4 peppercorns, a pinch of mace and a *bouquet garni*. Simmer gently for 50 minutes, strain liquid, press vegetables to extract all liquid, add seasoning and use as directed.

BÉCHAMEL SAUCE

1 oz. butter
1 oz. flour
¾ pint milk (or milk stock)

seasoning
lemon juice

Make a roux by melting the fat in a small saucepan and adding the flour, stirring over a gentle heat until the fat and the flour form a paste. Stir liquid in gradually, bringing slowly to the boil and stirring continually, add seasoning and simmer gently for 5 minutes. Remove from heat, add a dash of lemon juice.

By adding different ingredients to this basic recipe, various sauces can be made as follows:

AURORE SAUCE

Add ½ gill tomato pulp.

MUSHROOM SAUCE

Add 4 oz. peeled and chopped button mushrooms, previously cooked in a little butter. A tablespoon of cream enhances the flavour.

MORNAY SAUCE

Add 3 oz. grated cheese, preferably Gruyère, with ½ teaspoon prepared mustard.

SOUBISE SAUCE

Add 8 oz. of sieved, cooked onions.

EGG SAUCE

Add 2 sieved hard-boiled eggs.

PARSLEY SAUCE

Add 1 tablespoon finely chopped parsley.

CELERY SAUCE

Add 2 heads of cooked and sieved celery.

VELOUTÉ SAUCE

Velouté sauce is made like béchamel sauce, but substitute meat stock for the milk. The stock can be either chicken stock, veal stock or fish stock, but it must be good and well-flavoured.

CAPER SAUCE

Use fish stock adding two teaspoons of capers with a dessert-spoon of vinegar, or lemon juice.

ANCHOVY SAUCE

Add 3 teaspoons of anchovy essence (the stock can be half fish stock if desired).

BUTTER SAUCES

Under this heading come hollandaise, mousseline and choron sauces.

HOLLANDAISE SAUCE

4 tablespoons wine vinegar   2 eggs
4 oz butter   seasoning

Rapidly boil vinegar in a saucepan until 1 tablespoon remains. Beat egg yolks with a knob butter and add to vinegar. Place this in a double saucepan, add pinch salt, stirring continuously until yolks begin to thicken. Add pieces of butter gradually, making sure yolks do not curdle. Season delicately. This sauce should be served lukewarm, usually with salmon or asparagus.

CHORON SAUCE

As for hollandaise, but using white wine instead of vinegar. Whilst cooking, add 1 dessertspoon cream and 1 teaspoon lemon juice.

MOUSSELINE SAUCE

2 egg yolks   1 tablespoon whipped cream
3 oz. butter   salt and pepper to taste
1 dessertspoon lemon juice

In a double saucepan place the beaten egg yolks, lemon juice, seasoning and a knob of butter. Stir continuously until mixture begins to thicken and whisk in rest of butter. Cook very gently until thick and just before serving carefully fold in whipped cream.

This sauce is exceptionally nice with grilled salmon or grilled sole.

BREAD SAUCE

½ pint chicken stock
2 oz. soft breadcrumbs
1 onion

1 oz. margarine
seasoning

Peel and cut onion very finely and fry in fat until golden brown. Add stock and breadcrumbs, season well and cook very gently until the breadcrumbs swell, stirring frequently.

APPLE SAUCE

2 lb. cooking apples
sugar

water
1 oz. margarine

Peel, core and slice apples and simmer in as little water as possible, adding enough sugar to taste. Add margarine and cook until fruit is very soft. Drain and sieve.
    Serve with duck or goose.

CURRY SAUCE

1 oz. fat or margarine
1 small onion
1 small cooking apple
1 oz. flour
1 garlic clove (optional)

1 large teaspoon curry powder
1¾ pints vegetable or meat stock
2 teaspoons sugar
1 tablespoon lemon juice
a few sultanas (optional)

Melt fat in saucepan and cook gently for a few minutes the grated apple and chopped onion with the garlic. Add the curry powder and cook for 5 minutes over very low heat. Add the flour to form a roux, then the liquid, seasoning, lemon juice and sugar and simmer for 10 minutes. Add sultanas.

TOMATO SAUCE (1)

1 oz. margarine	1½ lb. tomatoes (tinned or fresh)
1 onion	1 small glass white wine
2 small carrots	little sugar
	seasoning

Peel and dice onion and carrots and cook in melted fat in a saucepan for 4 minutes. Add tomatoes (skinned if fresh), wine, seasoning, and simmer gently for 30 minutes. Put through a fine sieve, adding more sugar if required.

TOMATO SAUCE (2)

2 lb. tomatoes (tinned or fresh)	4 oz. minced beef
seasoning, including little sugar	1 oz. fat
1 onion	

Peel and cut onion very finely and cook gently in fat in a saucepan. Add tomatoes (peeled if fresh), seasoning and the meat. Simmer for 45 minutes and adjust seasoning.

This sauce is always served with spaghetti or ravioli (kreplech).

Add 1 dessertspoon Worcestershire sauce for a piquant flavour.

HORSERADISH SAUCE

1 horseradish root	white vinegar
little sugar	salt
½ cooked beetroot	

Clean horseradish and grate very finely. Place in a jar, cover with vinegar and add a little sugar and salt to taste. Mix in the finely grated beetroot (peeled).

Always serve this with gefillte fish.

MAYONNAISE

2 egg yolks
½ teaspoon each of mustard,
    sugar, and salt

pinch pepper
½ pint finest olive oil
white wine vinegar

Into a large bowl, place seasonings and egg yolks, stirring rapidly and continuously. Add oil, literally drop by drop. It is the oil which thickens the mixture, but if it is added too quickly, the mayonnaise will curdle. Add a little vinegar during the process and finally more vinegar if necessary. To make mayonnaise lighter in texture if desired, a little boiling water can be added at the end.

An interesting addition can be made to this sauce by adding 3 tomatoes, skinned and sieved.

FRENCH DRESSING

Beat until absolutely smooth a pinch of salt, pepper, dry mustard, 1 tablespoon lemon juice and 1 dessertspoon olive oil.

Add slowly 3 tablespoons more oil and, if desired, a little more lemon juice.

TARTARE SAUCE

½ pint mayonnaise
1 hard-boiled egg

1 tablespoon capers
1 small pickled gherkin

Sieve egg, chop gherkin finely and with the capers add to the mayonnaise.

SWEET SAUCES

JAM SAUCE

Allow 1 tablespoon any desired jam per person. Heat jam with 1 tablespoon water over gentle heat and use as desired.

LEMON SAUCE (1)

½ pint water   2 oz. sugar
2 tablespoons lemon juice ¾ oz. cornflour

Make a paste with cornflour and a little water. Bring remainder of water and other ingredients to the boil, add cornflour mixture and simmer for 5 minutes, stirring occasionally.

LEMON SAUCE (2) FLUFFY

½ pint water   2 oz. sugar
2 tablespoons lemon juice 2 egg yolks
1 tablespoon cornflour

Bring the water, sugar and lemon juice to the boil. Make a paste of the cornflour with a little cold water add to the sauce. Simmer until sauce thickens, stirring continuously. Pour over the well beaten yolks and mix thoroughly.

HARD SAUCE

4 oz. unsalted butter 2 tablespoons brandy
4 oz. icing sugar

Cream butter and sugar together until very creamy. Beat the brandy in gradually. Place in a small dish and chill until hard. Serve cut in wedges.
 Brandy can be replaced by rum, sherry or fruit juice.

CUSTARD SAUCE

½ pint milk   2 oz. sugar
1 egg and 1 egg yolk pinch salt

Whisk egg and yolk with the sugar and salt until thick and creamy. Add slightly warmed milk. Transfer to the top of a double boiler and stir continuously until mixture thickens.

CHOCOLATE SAUCE (1)

½ pint water   2 oz. sugar
3 oz. chocolate   ½ oz. cornflour

Put ¼ pint water, grated chocolate and sugar in a saucepan and cook gently until chocolate has melted. Bring to the boil, add cornflour mixed with the rest of the water. Boil gently, stirring continuously until thick.

CHOCOLATE SAUCE (2)

½ pint milk   2 oz. sugar
2 egg yolks   1 tablespoon cocoa
               or chocolate powder

Whisk egg yolks and sugar until thick and creamy. Dissolve chocolate or powder in the slightly warmed milk, add egg mixture and cook over a very gentle heat until mixture thickens, stirring continuously.

BRANDY, RUM OR SHERRY SAUCE

¾ pint milk or water   1 oz. butter or margarine
1 oz. cornflour   ½ gill desired spirit
2 oz. sugar

Mix cornflour with a little of the liquid. Bring remaining liquid to the boil, add cornflour mixture and sugar and boil for 1 minute, stirring continuously. Add spirit and butter and simmer for 3 or 4 minutes, continuing to stir. More sugar or spirit can be added according to taste.

PASTRY, PIES AND STRUDELS

There are few things more tempting or more reminiscent of the warm comforts of home than a kitchen filled with fragrance of freshly baked pastry. And who can resist the temptation of a juicy fruit pie or a superb strudel just emerging from the oven!

The making of good pastry, whether plain or in the more fancy varieties, is something which can be learned by every housewife, providing one follows a few simple rules.

All utensils should be cold and dry.

Always roll pastry in one direction, as lightly as possible, and never roll off the pastry.

Never stretch pastry, except in very special cases, e. g. Strudel pastry.

Fats used for making pastry can be butter, margarine, cooking fat, suet or corn oil.

Always use plain flour.

TO BAKE BLIND (EMPTY)

Line a greased dish with pastry and cover with greaseproof paper, pressing it down gently into all corners. Fill up with a layer of breadcrusts or haricot beans. (It is a good idea to keep a jar of beans solely for this purpose.) Bake in hot oven for 15 minutes. Remove from oven, lift out paper and beans or breadcrusts, return to moderate oven and bake for a further 10 minutes, until golden.

TO GLAZE PASTRY

All dessert pastry dishes should be glazed before putting them into the oven as this gives them an attractive appearance.

Slightly beat an egg and with a pastry brush paint the top of the pastry. Sprinkle with castor sugar and cook as directed.

SHORT PASTRY

(For pies and tarts)

8 oz. flour	pinch salt
4 oz. fat	cold water

Sieve flour and salt into a bowl and add fat cut into tiny pieces. Using only finger tips rub together until mixture resembles fine breadcrumbs. With a palette knife in one hand and a jug of cold water in the other, slowly pour in sufficient water, mixing with the knife until a fairly stiff paste is formed. On a lightly floured board, knead for a few minutes until pastry is free from all cracks.

RICH SHORT PASTRY

8 oz. flour
5 oz. butter
1 tablespoon castor sugar

1 egg
1 dessertspoon lemon juice
little cold water

Sieve flour, salt and sugar into a bowl. Add fat and proceed as for short pastry, but using lemon juice and beaten egg as liquid. If more liquid is required, add a little cold water. If this recipe is used for savoury dishes, the sugar will be omitted and a pinch of salt added.

CHOUX PASTRY

(For cream buns, éclairs, etc.)

4 oz. flour
2 oz. butter

$\frac{1}{4}$ pint water
2—3 eggs
pinch salt

Place fat and water in a saucepan and bring to fast boil. Add sieved flour and salt and stir quickly, then continue cooking and stirring until ball is formed and leaves sides of saucepan quite clean. Leave to cool. Beat in eggs one at a time, stirring continuously. Add only enough eggs to make paste smooth and shiny.

SUET CRUST

8 oz. flour
4 oz. finely chopped suet
cold water

pinch salt or 1 tablespoon
sugar according to the
dish

Proceed as for short crust (see page 114).
For steamed suet puddings, a lighter result is obtained by replacing half the flour with the same amount of soft bread-crumbs.

PUFF PASTRY

8 oz. flour	pinch salt
8 oz. butter	iced water

Sieve flour and salt into a bowl, rub in a knob of butter and sufficient water to make a firm dough. Manipulate remaining butter with the hands until it is the same consistency as the pastry. Roll out pastry on a cold board or enamel surface, lightly floured, to $\frac{3}{4}$ inch thick. Place remaining butter in centre and fold pastry over, sealing well. Roll into a long strip and fold as in rough puff pastry. Put into cold place for 15 minutes and repeat process, rolling, folding and chilling seven times in all, making sure that the open edge is always to the left.

ROUGH PUFF PASTRY

9 oz. flour	1 teaspoon lemon juice
6 oz. butter or margarine	cold water

Cut fat into flour. Add lemon juice and just sufficient water to make a firm, pliable dough. Wrap in greaseproof paper and chill for 15 minutes. Roll into a strip 1 inch thick and 5 inches wide and bring bottom end two thirds up and then fold the top end over. Turn dough so that the open edge is to the left and roll out again into a long strip. Fold as previously and chill again for 15 minutes.

If the pastry is not being used immediately, it should be chilled before using.

FLAKY PASTRY

8 oz. flour   cold water
5 oz. fat   pinch salt

Divide fat into four equal pieces. Sieve flour and salt into a bowl and add one portion of fat cut into small pieces. Mix to a firm dough with sufficient cold water and roll into a long strip. Place another portion of fat cut into small pieces over the top two thirds of the pastry, leaving $\frac{3}{4}$ inch margin. Fold as directed for rough puff pastry. Leave in a cool place for 15 minutes and repeat process twice using other two portions of fat. Chill before using.

KUCHEN DOUGH

1 lb. plain flour $\frac{1}{2}$ oz. yeast
2 oz. castor sugar   2 oz. butter or margarine
$\frac{1}{2}$ pint milk   1 egg

In a warm basin cream yeast with 1 teaspoon of sugar. In a saucepan melt fat in the milk and when lukewarm pour it on the creamed yeast. Place sieved flour and salt into another warm basin, make a well in the centre and pour in yeast mixture. With a spoon work in the flour and knead to a pliable dough. Cover with warm cloth and leave in warm place for 2 hours. Now add sugar and well beaten egg and knead well. Cover again with a warm cloth and set aside in warm place to rise again for 2 hours. The dough is now ready to use.

VOL-AU-VENT

puff pastry (see page 116)   egg white

Roll out pastry into rounds the size of a tea saucer. With medium sized biscuit cutter, indent pastry rounds two thirds into the depth, making sure not to cut deeper. Brush over with slightly beaten egg white and bake in very hot oven for 30 minutes. Remove from oven and when cool, remove centres and scoop out any pieces of uncooked pastry.

Fill as desired. Minced mushrooms, meat, chicken or fruits are all very good.

APPLE PIE

2 lb. cooking apples   lemon juice
rich short pastry (see page 115) sultanas (optional)
sugar   cinnamon
butter or margarine

Roll pastry rather thin and line greased pie dish. Slice peeled and cored apples and cook them in a very little water and lemon juice until pulpy, adding sugar to taste and sultanas, if used. Drain off excess juice, and when cool put into pastry lined dish. Sprinkle with a little cinnamon, dot with few pieces of butter or margarine and cover with top crust of pastry, making sure edges are well sealed. Make two or three slits in centre of top crust, and decorate with two or three pastry leaves. Bake in hot oven for 10 minutes, then reduce heat to moderate and continue cooking for 30 minutes more.

APPLE DESSERT PIE

rich short pastry (see page 115)
2 lb. cooking apples
2 eggs

½ pint milk
brown sugar
2 oz. castor sugar

Line a greased pie dish with pastry. Peel, core and slice apples and place neatly in the dish. Sprinkle well with brown sugar. Beat eggs well, add milk and 2 oz. castor sugar and beat again. Pour this over apples and bake in moderate oven for 40 minutes until set.

APPLE CUSTARD PIE

short pastry (see page 114)
2 lb. cooking apples
sugar

milk
2 eggs

Line a greased pie dish with pastry. Cook apples as directed and when cooked put through a sieve. Measure purée and make up to one pint with milk. Add the eggs beaten and mix thoroughly. Pour into dish and cook in moderate oven for about 40 minutes until custard is set.

CRISPY APPLE PIE

Proceed as for apple pie (see page 118), but just prior to placing pie in oven, spread very thin layer of golden syrup over top of pastry.

Bake as for Apple pie.

BAKEWELL TART

flaky or rich short crust
(see pages 117, 115)
2 eggs
3 oz. ground almonds

2 oz. castor sugar
raspberry jam
2 oz. butter or margarine

Line individual greased patty tins with pastry. Cream fat and sugar until white and creamy, add beaten eggs and beat, then add almonds and mix thoroughly. Put 1 teaspoon jam in each tin, fill with the almond mixture to ¼ inch from the top and bake in a moderate oven for 35 minutes.

CHOCOLATE PIE

short crust (see page 114)
2 oz. grated chocolate
1 oz. sugar

2 eggs
½ pint milk

Line a greased pie dish and bake blind (empty). Leave to get cold. Melt chocolate in a saucepan over gentle heat, add milk, sugar and beaten eggs and mix thoroughly. Pour into pastry case and bake in moderate oven for 35 minutes, or until chocolate custard is set.

CUSTARD PIE

short pastry (see page 114)
½ pint milk

2 eggs
2 oz. sugar

Beat eggs, sugar and milk thoroughly. Pour into a greased tin lined with pastry and bake in moderate oven until the custard is set, approximately 30 minutes.

LEMON CHIFFON PIE

rich short pastry
  (see page 115)
2 eggs
3 oz. castor sugar

grated rind of lemon
2 dessertspoons lemon juice
$\frac{1}{2}$ oz. gelatine, powdered
2 tablespoons whipped cream

Line a greased pie plate with rolled out pastry and bake blind (empty). Separate yolks from whites or eggs. Whisk yolks with sugar until thick and creamy. Add lemon juice, rind, dissolved gelatine and whisk until on point of setting. Fold in cream and stiffly beaten egg whites. Pour into pastry case and leave in cold place until set firm.

CHOCOLATE CHIFFON PIE

Proceed as for Lemon Chiffon pie, but substitute 2 oz. melted chocolate for the lemon rind and juice.

COCONUT TART

flaky or short crust
  (see pages 117, 114)
2 oz. butter or margarine
2 oz. sugar

2 eggs
1 oz. flour
2 oz. coconut

Grease a pie dish and line with pastry. Cream fat and sugar until white and creamy, add eggs and beat thoroughly. Gently fold in flour and coconut and fill pastry-lined pie dish. Cook in a moderate oven for 35 minutes.

LEMON MERINGUE PIE

rich short pastry
(see page 115)
½ pint water
4 oz. sugar

grated rind and
juice of 1 lemon
1 oz. cornflour
3 eggs

Line a greased pie dish with pastry and bake blind (empty). Leave until cool. Blend cornflour with a little cold water into a smooth paste. Boil rest of water, add cornfllour, 2 oz. sugar, rind and juice of the lemon. Bring to boil and simmer for 3 minutes, stirring continuously, making sure mixture is perfectly smooth. When cool add one egg and 2 egg yolks well beaten, mixing thoroughly. Cook over gentle heat for 2 minutes, stirring well. When mixture is cool and absolutely smooth, turn into baked pastry case and top with meringue made from remaining egg white stiffly beaten with remaining sugar. Bake in a slow oven for 20—25 minutes until meringue is set and pale golden.

CHOCOLATE MERINGUE PIE

Proceed as for lemon meringue pie, but substitute 3 oz. melted chocolate for lemon rind and juice.

MERINGUE PIES

short pastry (see page 114)
fruit filling

2 egg whites
2 oz. castor sugar

Any soft fruit may be used, e. g. apples, gooseberries, plums, etc. Cook fruit with sugar in very little water and cool. Place in a baked pastry shell. Beat egg whites stiffly and fold in castor sugar. Spread meringue over fruit, making sure it is completely covered. Cook in a slow oven for 20—25 minutes.

JAM TART

short pastry (see page 114)   jam

Line greased pie plate with rolled out pastry and spread with desired jam. Decorate top with thin strips of pastry and bake in a moderate oven for 30 minutes.

JAM PUFFS

puff pastry (see page 116)   jam

Roll out pastry ¼ inch thick and cut into 4-inch circles. Place teaspoon jam in centre of each circle and fold over, making absolutely certain edges are well sealed. Place on a baking sheet and cook in hot oven for 15 minutes.

APPLE TURNOVERS

flaky pastry or rich short crust (see pages 117, 115)   sugar
2 lb. cooking apples

Cook peeled, cored and sliced apples in a very little water with sugar to taste. When soft, put through a sieve. Roll out pastry ¼ inch thick and cut into circles of 3 inches. Place a dessertspoon of apple in centre and fold over, making sure edges are well sealed. Place on greased baking sheet and bake in a moderate oven 35 minutes for rich short crust pastry or 25 minutes in a hot oven for flaky pastry.

TREACLE TART

short crust pastry (see page 114)
3 oz. breadcrumbs

1 teaspoon lemon juice
4 tablespoons golden syrup

Line greased pie plate with rolled out pastry. Slightly warm the syrup, add lemon juice and breadcrumbs and mix thoroughly. Spread over pastry-lined plate, cover with strips of pastry, and bake in moderate oven for 40 minutes.

MINCE PIES

rough puff or flaky pastry (see pages 116, 117)   mincemeat

Line greased individual patty tins with thinly rolled out pastry. Fill with mincemeat and cover with a 'lid' of rolled pastry, making sure edges are well sealed. Make slits in top of pastry and bake in a moderate oven for about 25 minutes.

FRUIT FLANS

rich short crust (see page 115)
fruit

fruit syrup or apricot glaze

Line greased flan ring with rolled out pastry and cook blind (empty). Leave until cold. Any fresh or tinned fruit can be used or a combination of fruits. Arrange fruit attractively in the flan case. Pour over prepared syrup or apricot glaze and leave until set.

SYRUP FOR FRUIT FLANS

Use ¼ pint syrup obtained from either tinned fruit or fresh cooked fruit; add more sugar if desired and bring to the boil. Add 1 teaspoon arrowroot or cornflour mixed to a paste with a little cold water. Stir till boiling and simmer for 3 to 4 minutes.

APRICOT GLAZE

3 tablespoons apricot jam
¼ pint fruit juice

2 teaspoons cornflour
or arrowroot

Sieve the jam, add juice and bring to the boil. Add arrowroot or cornflour mixed to a paste with little cold water. Bring to the boil again, stir and simmer for 3 to 4 minutes.

CREAM SLICES

puff or flaky pastry
(see pages 116, 117)
raspberry jam

double cream (whipped)
white glacé icing
(see page 163)

Roll out pastry ⅛ inch thick and cut into strips 6 inches by 2½ inches. Place on baking sheet and bake in a very hot oven for 15 minutes. Remove from oven and leave to cool. Spread one piece of pastry with thin layer of jam, top with another piece of pastry and spread this with a fairly thick layer of whipped cream. Cover with third piece of pastry and spread with the glacé icing.

PASTRY FOR STRUDELS

2 cups flour
½ cup lukewarm water
1 tablespoon best cooking oil

1 egg
pinch salt

Sift flour on to a board in a heap. Mix together the water, oil, egg and salt and pour this mixture into the centre of the flour, stirring with a knife until well mixed. Knead and cover with warm basin for 20 minutes. Spread a clean white tablecloth over the table and dust with flour. Place dough in centre and roll out as thinly as possible but without breaking the pastry Place your two hands, with the fingers curled into the palms. under the pastry and with the back of the hands gently pull and stretch the dough until it is paper thin. On no account must the pastry be torn.

ALMOND STRUDEL

8 oz. ground almonds
4 egg yolks
½ cup castor sugar

grated peel of lemon
little oil
strudel pastry (see above)

Beat egg yolks and sugar until light and thick. Add almonds and lemon rind. Prepare strudel pastry and when stretched brush over with a little oil. Spread almond mixture over pastry and roll up as for a jam roll. Bake as for apple strudel (see page 127).

CHERRY STRUDEL

2 lb. morella cherries   1 cup sugar
½ cup breadcrumbs   4 oz. ground almonds
½ teaspoon cinnamon   grated peel of a lemon
little oil   Strudel pastry (see page 126)

Stem and pit cherries and add all other ingredients. Prepare strudel pastry and when stretched brush over with a little oil. Spread cherry mixture evenly over pastry and roll up as for a jam roll. Bake as for apple strudel (see below).

APPLE STRUDEL

2 lb. cooking apples   1 cup sugar
½ cup sultanas   1 teaspoon cinnamon
½ cup ground almonds   cooking oil

Peel, core and chop the apples. Mix them with all other ingredients (except oil) and spread evenly over the dough. Sprinkle this lightly with oil. Roll a few inches of dough over apple mixture, then hold one end of the cloth high with both hands and the strudel will literally roll itself over and over into a roll. Place in a fairly large greased shallow baking tin, bending the strudel very carefully to fit round the tin. Bake in moderate oven about 45 minutes until brown and crisp. Baste occasionally with a little oil.

CHOCOLATE ÉCLAIRS

choux pastry (see page 115)   whipped cream
                                melted chocolate

Place choux pastry in a piping bag with $\frac{1}{2}$ inch nozzle and force mixture on to greased baking sheet in 4-inch lengths. Bake in moderate oven for 35 minutes. Remove from oven and with sharp knife make a slit along the sides and leave to cool. When cold force whipped cream into the éclairs through the slits, and with hot knife spread melted chocolate over the top.

CREAM BUNS

Proceed as for chocolate éclairs, but pipe the pastry into small mounds.
   Sprinkle tops with icing sugar instead of chocolate.

STEAMED, BAKED AND MILK PUDDINGS

Particularly with a growing family, the serving of a delicious sweet is not only an enjoyable but an essential way of ending a meal. The variety is endless, and choice will depend on individual tastes and appetites. One may choose the delicate blancmange or custard, the light milk pudding, particularly beneficial to children and invalids, or the delicious lockshen pudding or jam roly poly, always so satisfying to hearty young appetites.

Very often the preceding courses of a meal will suggest a steamed or baked pudding and if the oven is in use, this is also an economical opportunity to have a baked pudding.

TO STEAM PUDDINGS

Fill basin only two thirds to allow mixture to rise. Cover with greased paper and then with a scalded cloth. Tie cloth round top of basin with a piece of string. The ends of the cloth can be brought up and tied and this will act as a handle when removing basin from steamer when pudding is cooked. If one does not possess a steamer, place a colander on top of a saucepan, making sure it fits tightly. Place pudding basin in colander and cover with a tightly fitting lid. Water in saucepan should never at any time be off the boil and it is advisable to check every 30 minutes to ascertain if more water is required, and this, of course, must be boiling when added.

LAYER PUDDINGS

8 oz. suet pastry or short pastry (see pages 115, 114)

fresh fruit
sugar

Roll pastry into rounds $\frac{1}{8}$ inch thick and line greased pudding basin with one round. Put layer of the desired fruit in this and sprinkle with sugar (lemon juice etc., for some recipes). Lay another round of pastry on top and repeat layers, finishing with pastry, making sure edges are well sealed. Steam for 3 hours.

APPLE LAYER PUDDING

1½ lb. cooking apples
suet or short pastry
(see pages 115, 114)
1 tablespoon golden syrup

2 oz. sugar
2 oz. sultanas
2 oz. cake crumbs
1 tablespoon lemon juice

Peel, core and chop apples and mix thoroughly with all other ingredients except pastry. Roll pastry into rounds and line a greased pudding basin. Fill with alternative layers of apple mixture and pastry, finishing with pastry. Steam for 3 hours.

STEAMED FRUIT PUDDING

8 oz. suet pastry　　any desired fresh fruit
　(see page 115)　　suitable for puddings
sugar

Roll out pastry $\frac{1}{4}$ inch thick and with two thirds of pastry line greased pudding basin. Fill with desired fruit, adding sugar between each layer according to tartness of fruit, and $\frac{1}{2}$ cup water. Cover with remaining pastry, making sure edges are well sealed. Steam for 2 hours.

APPLE PUDDING (1)

Proceed as for steamed fruit pudding, using peeled, cored and sliced apples as the fruit.

APPLE PUDDING (2)

2 lb. cooking apples　　　3 oz. sugar
3 oz. bread or cake crumbs 2 eggs
a few sultanas　　　　　1 tablespoon lemon juice

Peel core and cut apples into small pieces. Beat eggs lightly and mix with all ingredients very thoroughly. Turn into a greased basin and steam for 2 hours.

CANARY PUDDING

4 oz. plain flour	4 oz. fat
1 teaspoon baking powder	4 oz. sugar
pinch salt	2 eggs

Cream sugar and fat thoroughly, add slightly beaten eggs and cream together for 3 or 4 minutes until light and fluffy. Fold in sieved flour, salt and baking powder and use as follows:

Jam Pudding. Place 3 tablespoons stoneless jam at the bottom of a greased basin and cover with the mixture.

Apples. Place a thick layer of peeled, cored and chopped apples in basin.

Mixed fruits. Mixture of chopped figs and raisins. Chopped dates and apples etc.

Chocolate. Replace 1 oz. flour with 1 oz. cocoa.

Steam puddings for 2½ hours.

Individual basins can be used (these are known as *Castle Puddings*), but steam for 2 hours only.

PLUM PUDDING

4 oz. flour	4 oz. suet
6 oz. fresh breadcrumbs	4 oz. sultanas and currants
4 oz. sugar	mixed
2 eggs	1 gill fruit juice
1 teaspoon mixed spice	1 teaspoon lemon juice

Mix flour, suet, breadcrumbs, sugar, washed and dried fruit and spice well together. Add well beaten eggs, fruit and lemon juice and beat into dry mixture. Turn into well-greased basin and steam for 3½ hours.

ROLY POLY

8 oz. suet pastry (see page 115)   filling (see below)

Roll out pastry into an oblong $\frac{1}{3}$ inch thick and spread with any of the following as desired, leaving a margin of 1 inch all round. Roll up like a Swiss roll and place in floured cloth (previously scalded and dried) allowing room for pastry to swell. Tie ends securely and boil in deep saucepan of boiling water for 3 hours.

Fillings. Spread pastry with jam

or peeled, cored and finely chopped apples sweetened with sugar.

or spread with golden syrup and then sprinkle with fresh breadcrumbs or stale cake crumbs.

BAKED PUDDING

4 oz. flour	2 oz. fat
2 eggs	2 oz. sugar
	pinch salt

Cream fat and sugar thoroughly, add slightly beaten eggs and beat for few minutes. Carefully fold in sieved flour. Place desired fruit in greased baking dish, cover with cake mixture and bake in moderate oven for 50 minutes.

Suggested fruits. Chopped dates and apples.

Cover bottom of dish with pitted, stemmed cherries or pitted tinned cherries.

Layer of stewed fruit.

BAKED RICE PUDDING

1½ oz. short rice	1 oz. sugar
1 pint milk	pinch salt
1 oz. butter or margarine	

Place the washed rice in greased dish, pour over the slightly warmed milk to which has been added butter, sugar and salt. Bake in slow oven for 3 hours, stirring at intervals.

SAGO AND TAPIOCA PUDDING

Proceed as for *Rice Pudding*, but allow filled pie dish to stand 1 hour before baking.

LOCKSHEN PUDDING

6 oz. cooked and drained lockshen (see page 35)	3 oz. sugar
2 eggs	2 oz. sultanas
1 oz. ground almonds	1 oz. margarine or chicken fat
1 dessertspoon lemon juice	

Beat eggs lightly and mix with all other ingredients. Turn into greased ovenproof dish and bake in moderate oven for 45 minutes or steam in basin for 1½ hours.

BREAD PUDDING

1 lb. stale white bread
2 eggs
1 oz. melted margarine
3 oz. sugar

6 oz. sultanas
1 teaspoon mixed spice
3 large tablespoons orange
    marmalade

Cut bread in pieces and soak in cold water until soft and pulpy. Drain and squeeze very thoroughly until absolutely dry. Add all other ingredients, mixing thoroughly. Turn into a greased baking dish and bake in a moderate oven for $1\frac{1}{2}$ hours.

The addition of marmalade makes this pudding something out of the ordinary.

BREAD AND BUTTER PUDDING

2 slices thinly cut bread
    and butter
2 tablespoons sultanas
$1\frac{1}{2}$ oz. sugar

$\frac{1}{2}$ pint milk
1 egg
1 egg yolk

Grease pie dish and place in it the bread and butter, and sprinkle with sultanas. Slightly warm the milk, add beaten egg, yolk and sugar and stir thoroughly. Pour this over bread and allow to stand for 30 minutes. Place dish in another dish half filled with cold water and cook in moderate oven for 40 minutes.

QUEEN PUDDING

¾ pint milk
4 oz. sugar
3 oz. fresh white
   breadcrumbs

juice and rind
  of 1 lemon
knob butter
3 eggs
jam

Place lemon rind in a bowl and pour over heated milk. Cover bowl and allow to stand for 30 minutes. Strain milk and add 1½ oz. sugar, butter, breadcrumbs and stir until butter is melted. Leave until quite cool. Slightly beat 2 egg yolks and 1 whole egg and add to milk mixture. Pour into greased deep pie dish and place in pan half filled with cold water. Bake in moderate oven for 40 minutes. Remove from oven and when cool spread a thin layer of jam over top (jam will spread easily if it is slightly warmed). Make meringue with 2 stiffly beaten egg whites and remaining sugar. Spread roughly over top, return dish to slow oven and bake 20 minutes, or until meringue is set and lightly coloured.

APPLE CHARLOTTE

2 lb. cooking apples
2 oz. sugar
6 oz. stale bread or cake crumbs

1 tablespoon lemon juice
1 tablespoon golden syrup
1 tablespoon water

Into a greased oven dish put a layer of crumbs, then layer of peeled and thinly sliced apples and repeat until dish is full, finishing with layer of crumbs. Place all other ingredients in a saucepan and stir over gentle heat until sugar is dissolved. Pour this syrup over the dish and bake in a fairly moderate oven for 1½ hours.

APPLE CRUMBLE

2 lb. cooking apples	lemon juice
sugar	2 oz. sugar
4 oz. flour	2 oz. butter or margarine

Peel, core and slice apples and cook as for apple pie (see page 118). Place in a pie dish. Put flour and 2 oz. sugar in bowl, add fat cut into small pieces and rub together until it resembles fine breadcrumbs. Spoon mixture over hot apples about 1 inch deep and bake in moderate oven for 35 minutes.

Note. Any soft well drained fruit can replace apples, i. e. plums, rhubarb, gooseberries, etc.

BAKED APPLES

1 large cooking apple per person	sultanas
(Bramley apples are best)	water
brown sugar	

Wash and cut a slice from top of each apple to make a 'lid'. Core apples and fill cavities tightly with sugar and a few sultanas, and replace 'lid'. Place apples in greased baking dish, pour over 1 teacup water in which has been dissolved 1 tablespoon sugar. Bake in a moderate oven until tender. Lift out carefully.

Cold sweets make a good finish to a meal on hot days and can often be made in advance, which is a great boon to the cook.

This type of sweet can be decorated in various ways, e. g. with whipped cream, glacé cherries or angelica, which not only make a party dish of the sweet but enhance the appearance of any table on which they are placed.

CRÈME BRULÉE

This is a popular party sweet, but rather expensive to make.

> 1 pint cream   4 egg yolks
> 3 oz. sugar

Whisk yolks with sugar until very thick and creamy, add cream and mix thoroughly. Place mixture in top of double saucepan and cook over hot but NOT boiling water until mixture thickens, stirring often. Care must be taken to see that the water does not get too hot or the mixture will curdle.

Pour into fireproof dish and leave to cool. When cool, spread a thin layer of castor sugar on top and place under hot grill for 2 *seconds* (watching carefully) until sugar caramelises.

CARAMEL CUSTARD

1 pint milk	3 oz. loaf sugar
2 eggs	2 tablespoons cold water
3 oz. castor sugar	

Place loaf sugar in thick saucepan and cook over gentle heat until dissolved and brown. Add water quickly and carefully as the sugar may splutter. Return to heat and cook until caramel is dark brown and very syrupy. Turn this into an ovenproof dish, turning it around quickly so as to coat the bottom and sides with caramel. Slightly warm milk, add castor sugar, beaten eggs and whisk thoroughly. Pour this into prepared dish, place dish in tin half filled with cold water and bake in moderate oven for 45 minutes.

This can also be made in small individual dishes.

The custard must be absolutely cold before turning out.

RICH CUSTARD

½ pint milk	2 oz. castor sugar
2 eggs	½ oz. gelatine
3 tablespoons cream	

Whisk eggs, add sugar and whisk until thick and very creamy. Add slightly warmed milk and cook over very gentle heat until mixture thickens. Add gelatine, dissolved in 1 tablespoon water and stir thoroughly. Just as the custard is on the point of setting, carefully fold in the whipped cream.

CHARLOTTE RUSSE

sponge fingers
½ pint jelly (lemon
   jelly is very nice)

rich custard (see page 139)
tinned fruit
angelica to decorate
cream

Pour thin layer of jelly into charlotte mould. Chill. When nearly set, line mould with sponge fingers, placing their ends in the jelly. Cover with layer of drained fruit and pour over remainder of jelly. When set pour over the rich custard, leave to set. Turn out on to serving dish and decorate with whipped cream and angelica.

SOUFFLÉS AND MOUSSES - HOT AND COLD

Probably in no other branch of cooking is the cook so apprehensive as in the making and cooking of hot soufflés. Yet as long as one follows the instructions carefully, there is very little chance of anything going wrong. The main points to observe are:

1. To follow the instructions implicitly.

2. Hot soufflés must be eaten immediately they are taken from the oven. The 'mighty' soufflé does not wait for anyone, and in fact, it is diners who must wait for the soufflé.

Cold mousses and soufflés are more or less the same, but a mousse usually contains less egg white and cream than a soufflé. Soufflés also make a good entrée and in some cases can be served as the main dish. Use meat or chicken stock instead of milk, and margarine instead of butter. Omit sugar and season with salt and pepper, and add desired ingredients. Suggestions: minced chicken, tongue, sweet corn, tomato purée.

BASIC RECIPE FOR SOUFFLÉ

2½ oz. butter	½ pint milk
2 oz. plain flour	3 eggs
2 oz. sugar	

Separate yolks and whites of the eggs. In a thick saucepan melt the butter, add flour and cook over gentle heat until roux is formed, blending well with a wooden spoon. Add milk and sugar and bring slowly to the boil, stirring continuously. Reduce heat and cook for full 3 minutes, stirring continually. Add flavouring (see recipes) and slightly beaten egg yolks. Cook over gentle heat for another minute and remove saucepan from heat. Whisk egg whites until stiff and fold them gently but thoroughly into the mixture. Pour this into greased 2-pint soufflé dish, place dish in pan half filled with cold water and bake in moderate oven for 45 minutes. *Note.* Never fill the dish more than two thirds full.

CHOCOLATE SOUFFLÉ

Dissolve 2 oz. chocolate in the milk before adding to the roux.

BANANA SOUFFLÉ

Add 2 peeled and mashed bananas to the mixture before adding the egg yolks.

APPLE SOUFFLÉ

Add 4 tablespoons of thick, sweetened apple purée before adding the egg yolks.
Note. Any purée of cooked sweetened fruit can be added to make a fruit soufflé.

COLD CHOCOLATE SOUFFLÉ

¾ pint milk	½ oz. gelatine
3 eggs	2½ oz. sugar
2 oz. chocolate	2 tablespoon double cream

Dissolve chocolate in the milk in saucepan over gentle heat. Separate egg yolks from whites and whisk yolks with sugar until thick and creamy. Add chocolate mixture and transfer to the top of double boiler (taking care water in bottom saucepan is not too hot) and stir until mixture thickens slightly. Dissolve gelatine in 2 tablespoons water or fruit juice (never use milk) and add to the egg mixture, stirring thoroughly. Leave in a cold place. *Just* as the mixture is beginning to set, gently and carefully fold in cream and stiffly beaten egg whites and leave to set.

To make into an attractive party dish: Turn out on to serving dish, decorate with whipped cream and pieces of flaked chocolate.

COFFEE SOUFFLÉ

Proceed as for cold chocolate soufflé. Omit chocolate and substitute 1 tablespoon coffee essence for 1 tablespoon of the milk.

ORANGE OR LEMON SOUFFLÉ

Proceed as for cold chocolate soufflé, but substitute lemon or orange juice with a little grated peel for the milk.

BLANCMANGE

1 pint milk	1½ oz. cornflour
1 tablespoon sugar	any desired flavouring
	1 egg

Make paste with cornflour and a little of the milk. Bring remainder of milk to the boil, add sugar and stir into cornflour. Return to saucepan and boil over gentle heat for 3 minutes, stirring continuously. When cool, add slightly beaten egg and mix thoroughly. Leave in cold place to set.

CHOCOLATE BLANCMANGE

Proceed as for blancmange, but dissolve 1 oz. of chocolate or 1 tablespoon cocoa, in the milk.

COFFEE BLANCMANGE

Proceed as for blancmange, but add 1 dessertspoon coffee essence to the milk.

TRIFLE

1 small stale sponge cake	fresh or tinned fruit as desired
2 tablespoons sherry	custard
	nuts and/or cream for decoration

Slice the cake and put into a dish. Pour over the sherry and leave for 1 hour. Make custard and pour half over the cake. Cool. When set, place a thick layer of the desired fruit on top and cover with remainder of custard. When set, decorate top of trifle with whipped cream, nuts (usually blanched and halved almonds) and pieces of fruit.

MERINGUES CHANTILLY

3 egg whites	thick cream
6 oz. castor sugar	pinch salt

Beat egg whites until stiff, add 2 tablespoons sugar and salt, whisk until very stiff, then gently fold in remainder of the sugar. Put mixture into a piping bag and pipe mounds on to sheets of greased paper (this can also be done with a tablespoon).

Cook in very slow oven for at least 2 hours and then leave to cool.

To serve. Sandwich 2 meringues together with whipped cream and place a wafer at the side of the dish. Additional cream can be handed round.

ZABAGLIONE (1)

4 eggs	½ cup sherry or fruit juice
3 oz. castor sugar	

Beat eggs until thick and creamy. Add sugar and whisk until thoroughly blended, then very slowly add sherry or fruit juice. Place mixture in top of double boiler over hot water (taking care water in bottom part of saucepan does not boil) and cook until mixture leaves sides of the pan, stirring continuously.

Remove from heat, mix again, and serve warm.

ZABAGLIONE (2)

4 egg yolks	3 oz. castor sugar
2 egg whites	¼ pint sherry

Whisk yolks and sugar until very thick and creamy. Add sherry gradually and cook in top of double boiler over gentle heat (taking care water does not boil in bottom part of saucepan).

When mixture has thickened, fold in the stiffly beaten egg whites.

Remove from heat, turn into a dish and leave until very cold.

BAKED ALASKA

1 sponge cake (sandwiched with jam and cream)	1 large block ice cream
	3 egg whites
2 bananas	5 oz. castor sugar

Place sponge cake on thick baking tray. Peel and slice bananas and place them on top of cake and then the ice cream on top of this, leaving a margin of ½ inch all round. Whisk the egg whites with 2 ounces of sugar until stiff and then carefully fold in remainder of sugar. Completely envelope the cake with meringue and place in pre-heated very hot oven for 4 minutes, until meringue is set. Serve immediately.

Note. The ice cream will NOT melt!

STRAWBERRY MOUSSE

3 eggs	3 oz. castor sugar
2 egg yolks	3 tablespoons crushed
2 tablespoons	strawberries
double cream	½ oz. gelatine

Whisk eggs, yolks and sugar in a saucepan over gentle heat until thick and creamy. Add fruit, and the gelatine dissolved in 1 tablespoon lemon juice, and stir thoroughly. Just as the mixture is on the point of setting, carefully fold in the cream. Pour into a dish and leave to set.

RASPBERRY MOUSSE

Proceed as for strawberry mousse, but substitute crushed raspberries. Many different mousses can be made by using any desired fruit purées.

LEMON OR ORANGE MOUSSE

3 eggs	lemon or orange juice
4 oz. sugar	½ oz. gelatine
4 tablespoons double cream	

Separate yolks from whites of the eggs. Whisk yolks and sugar in saucepan over gentle heat until thick and creamy. Add 2 tablespoons fresh lemon or orange juice, and the gelatine dissolved in 1 tablespoon of fruit juice, stirring well. Just as the mixture is beginning to set, gently and carefully fold in stiffly beaten egg whites and the cream. Leave to set.

FRUIT FOOL

1½ lb. any well sweetened   ½ pint cream, whipped
    cooked and sieved fruit

Fold cream carefully into the fruit purée. Place in refrigerator
until set. Serve with sponge fingers or wafer biscuits.

STRAWBERRY OR RASPBERRY FOOL

These fruits should, naturally, be mashed and sweetened.
Proceed as for Fruit Fool.

FRUIT SNOW

Proceed as for fruit fool, but omit cream and fold in 2 stiffly
beaten egg whites.

PEACHES IN SYRUP

Allow 1 ripe peach per person   ¼ pint water
1 teaspoon sherry or brandy   2 oz. sugar

Dissolve sugar in hot water in saucepan and boil gently until
syrupy. If it becomes too thick, add a little more water. Place
peaches (unpeeled) in the syrup and cook over very gentle
heat until the fruit is warmed through. Serve with little of
the syrup.

STEWED FRUITS

Fruit should be cooked gently, either in the oven in a casserole or in a saucepan on top of the stove. The fruit should be well washed before handling.

Apples, should be peeled, cored and sliced thinly.

Gooseberries should be topped and tailed.

Cherries, plums, etc. should be stalked.

Pears should be peeled, cored and quartered.

Rhubarb cut off leafy tops, and cut into $1\frac{1}{2}$ inch pieces.

Acid fruits require less sugar if $\frac{1}{2}$ teaspoon bicarbonate of soda is added while cooking.

Dried fruits. Wash well, cover with water and leave for several hours to soak. Cook in same water with sugar and little lemon according to taste. Prunes should always have little lemon added.

CAKES, SPONGES, ICINGS AND FILLINGS

If one desired to make a statement about cakes, it would be 'never could so much be done from so little.' From 2 or 3 eggs, a little flour, sugar, fat and a few extras, think of the fantastic number of cakes, gâteaux and sponges that can be produced.

For successful results, directions must be strictly followed. Have all the exact ingredients and have them and the bowls, etc. ready before starting to make the cake. Cake and sponge tins must be well greased and it is advisable when making rich fruit cakes to line the tin with greaseproof paper. The oven must be pre-heated to the correct temperature. Test a cake carefully to ascertain if it is cooked.

TO TEST CAKES

Sponge cakes. Press lightly on centre of cake. It should spring back immediately and the sides of the cake will have slightly shrunk from the sides of the tin.

Large cakes. A warm skewer inserted into the centre of the cake should come out perfectly clean.

Leave cake in the tin to cool before turning out on a wire tray so that the air can circulate around it.

TO STORE RICH FRUIT CAKES

When the cake is *absolutely* cold, prick the top in several places with a steel knitting needle. With the tip of a teaspoon drip sherry, rum or brandy into the holes. Enclose the cake *completely* in greaseproof paper, place in a cake tin and seal the tin with adhesive tape. The cake should keep fresh for 3 or 4 months.

PLAIN CAKE

6 oz. butter or margarine	6 oz. plain flour
6 oz. castor sugar	1 teaspoon baking powder
3 eggs	$\frac{1}{2}$ teaspoon vanilla essence

Cream fat and sugar thoroughly, add slightly beaten eggs, one at a time and beat until mixture is very thick and creamy. Carefully fold in flour sieved with baking powder and then the essence. Pour into well greased 7-inch tin and bake in moderate oven for $1\frac{1}{4}$ hours.

COCONUT CAKE

6 oz. butter or margarine	6 oz. plain flour
6 oz. castor sugar	1 teaspoon baking powder
3 eggs	1 cup finely shredded coconut
	½ teaspoon vanilla essence

Cream fat and sugar thoroughly, add slightly beaten eggs, one at a time and beat until mixture is very thick and creamy. Carefully fold in coconut, the flour sieved with baking powder and then the essence, blending well together. Pour into well greased 7-inch tin and bake in a moderate oven for 1¼ hours.

MARMALADE CAKE

6 oz. butter or margarine	6 oz. plain flour
6 oz. castor sugar	1 teaspoon baking powder
3 eggs	3 tablespoons marmalade

Cream fat and sugar thoroughly, add slightly beaten eggs, one at a time and beat until mixture is very thick and creamy. Beat in the marmalade. Carefully fold in flour sieved with baking powder, mixing lightly. Pour into well greased 7-inch tin and bake in moderate oven for 1¼ hours.

ORANGE CAKE

4 oz. butter	4 tablespoons orange juice
4 oz. castor sugar	grated rind of 1 orange
3 eggs	½ teaspoon baking powder
6 oz. plain flour	

Cream fat and sugar thoroughly, add slightly beaten eggs one at a time, then the orange rind and beat until mixture is thick and creamy. Carefully fold in flour sieved with baking powder, then the orange juice, and blend well. Pour into well greased 6-inch tin and bake in moderate oven for 1¼ hours.

CHOCOLATE CAKE (1)

6 oz. butter or margarine	1½ oz. cocoa
6 oz. castor sugar	½ teaspoon baking powder
3 eggs	4½ oz. plain flour

Cream fat and sugar thoroughly, add slightly beaten eggs, one at a time and beat until mixture is thick and creamy. Carefully fold in flour sieved with the baking powder and cocoa, mixing well. Pour into well greased 7-inch tin and bake in moderate oven for 1¼ hours.

CHOCOLATE CAKE (2)

4 oz. butter or margarine	5 oz. plain flour
4 oz. castor sugar	½ teaspoon baking powder
2 eggs	½ teaspoon vanilla essence
	2 oz. chocolate

Cream fat and sugar thoroughly, add slightly beaten eggs, one at a time and beat until mixture is thick and creamy. Melt chocolate in a saucepan over very gentle heat and to the mixture, blending thoroughly. Fold in flour sieved with baking powder, then the essence. Pour into 6-inch tin and bake in moderate oven for 1¼ hours.

ANGEL CAKE

5 egg whites	5 oz. castor sugar
½ teaspoon cream of tartar	1¾ oz. plain flour
1 dessertspoon cold water	¼ oz. cornflour

Beat the egg whites, cream of tartar and water until mixture is very stiff. Add sugar and beat for a further minute. Gently fold in sieved flours. Bake in 7-inch tin in a moderate oven for 40 minutes.

SULTANA CAKE

4 oz. butter or margarine	8 oz. plain flour
4 oz. castor sugar	½ teaspoon baking powder
2 eggs	6 oz. sultanas
1 teaspoon almond essence	

Cream fat and sugar thoroughly, add slightly beaten eggs, one at a time, and beat until mixture is very thick and creamy. Carefully fold in the flour sieved with baking powder, essence and lastly the fruit. Combine well, but gently. Pour into 6-inch tin and bake in moderate oven for 1¼ hours.

RICH FRUIT CAKE

10 oz. butter or margarine	12 oz. currants
10 oz. castor sugar	4 oz. chopped mixed peel
6 eggs	4 oz. glacé cherries
16 oz. sultanas	2 oz. chopped almonds
10 oz. plain flour	4 tablespoons sherry

Quarter cherries. Cream fat and sugar thoroughly together and add the slightly beaten eggs, one at a time, beating until thick and creamy. Fold in sieved flour, then fruits and nuts and lastly sherry. Blend thoroughly and add a little milk if necessary. Pour into well greased lined 10-inch cake tin and bake in slow oven for 3½ hours.

Cover the top of this cake, and any fruit cake that calls for long, slow cooking, with a piece of greaseproof paper after 1¾ hours cooking. This prevents the cake from browning too quickly.

WALNUT CAKE

6 oz. butter or margarine
6 oz. castor sugar
3 eggs

8 oz. plain flour
½ teaspoon baking powder
4 oz. chopped walnuts
a few halved walnuts

Cream fat and sugar thoroughly, add slightly beaten eggs, one at a time and beat until mixture is thick and creamy. Sieve flour with baking powder and add chopped nuts to this. Fold in very carefully to the egg mixture and pour into a 7-inch tin. Place the halved nuts on top and bake in moderate oven for 1¼ hours.

CHERRY CAKE

7 oz. butter or margarine
6 oz. castor sugar
3 eggs
4 oz. glazed cherries

9 oz. plain flour
1 teaspoon baking powder
1 teaspoon vanilla or almond essence

Cut cherries into quarters. (This is best done by covering them with a little flour so that they will not be sticky.)

Cream fat and sugar thoroughly, add slightly beaten eggs, one at a time and beat until mixture is thick and creamy. Fold in the flour sieved with baking powder, then cherries and essence.

This cake is nicest baked in an oblong tin. Bake in a moderate oven for 1¼ hours.

MADEIRA CAKE

5 oz. butter or margarine
5 oz. castor sugar
3 eggs
2 slices citron peel

8 oz. plain flour
1 teaspoon baking powder
½ teaspoon lemon essence
little milk (about 2 table-
    spoons)

Cream fat and sugar thoroughly and add slightly beaten eggs one at a time and beat until mixture is thick and creamy. Fold in flour sieved with baking powder, add essence and a little milk. Pour mixture into greased 7-inch tin and bake in moderate oven for 1½ hours. After 45 minutes, open oven door very carefully, place citron peel on top of cake and continue baking.

DUNDEE CAKE

8 oz. butter or margarine
8 oz. sugar
4 eggs
8 oz. sultanas
6 oz. currants

3 oz. chopped mixed peel
2 oz. glacé cherries
1 tablespoon lemon juice
8 oz. flour
2 oz. blanched, halved almonds

Quarter the cherries. Cream fat and sugar together and add slightly beaten eggs, one at a time. Carefully and thoroughly fold in sieved flour, fruit and lemon juice.

Line greased 9-inch cake tin with greaseproof paper and pour in the mixture. Place almonds over the top and bake in slow oven for 2½ to 3 hours.

CHEESE CAKE

1½ lb. cooking cheese
   (cream cheese)
1 cup sugar
3 eggs
¼ pint double cream

2 tablespoons flour
1 teaspoon lemon juice
pinch salt

The greased baking tin can either be lined with thinly rolled out short pastry, thinly cut sponge cake or cake or biscuit crumbs. The secret of a successful and delicious cheese cake is long beating and an electric beater is recommended. Place eggs and sugar in a large bowl and beat until very thick and creamy. In another bowl place cheese, flour, salt, lemon juice and cream and beat thoroughly. Combine contents of the two bowls and beat together. Pour mixture into prepared tin and bake in moderate oven for 1¼ hours. The cake will rise like a soufflé. Turn off heat in oven and let cake remain there for 20 minutes with oven door slightly open. This cake is a great favourite and is especially made for the Festival of Pentecost.

SEED CAKE

5 oz. butter or margarine
6 oz. castor sugar
3 eggs

8 oz. plain flour
½ teaspoon baking powder
2 teaspoons caraway seeds

Sieve flour with baking powder and add caraway seeds. Cream sugar and butter until thick and creamy and add slightly beaten eggs one at a time. Carefully fold in flour etc., and add a little milk if necessary. Pour into a well greased 7-inch cake tin and bake in moderate oven for 1 hour.

SAND CAKE

8 oz. butter   6 oz. cornflour
8 oz. castor sugar   2 oz. plain flour
4 eggs

Melt butter in saucepan over gentle heat. Separate yolks and
whites of eggs. Whisk whites until stiff, add sugar and beat for
1 minute. Add yolks and beat for a further 2 minutes. Gradually and carefully fold in flour and cornflour sieved together,
alternately with cooled, melted butter. Pour into well greased
8-inch tin and bake in moderate oven for 1 hour 20 minutes.

HONEY CAKE (LEKACH)

6 oz. castor sugar   12 oz. plain flour
2 eggs   1 teaspoon baking powder
$\frac{1}{2}$ cup oil   1 teaspoon ground ginger
8 oz. honey or golden syrup $\frac{1}{2}$ teaspoon mixed spice
blanched and halved almonds   1 teaspoon bicarbonate of
1 teacup warm water   soda

Cream sugar and eggs well, add oil and honey and mix
thoroughly. Sieve the flour with baking powder, ginger, spice,
bicarbonate of soda and add alternately with cup of warm
water to the honey mixture. Pour into greased floured tin,
decorate with the almonds and bake in moderate oven for
1 hour.

This is the traditional cake for the New Year Festival.

HAMANTASCHEN

Kuchen dough (see page 117)   fillings as below

Roll out dough ¼ inch thick, cut into 4-inch rounds and
brush with melted butter or margarine. Place 1 dessertspoon of filling in centre of each round and fold edges to
form a three cornered cake. Brush tops with warm melted
honey, leave in warm place until doubled in bulk.

Bake on greased tins in moderate oven until golden brown.

Poppy seed filling

4 oz. ground poppy seeds   2 oz. chopped nuts
1 cup milk   2 tablespoons golden
2 oz. butter or margarine   syrup

Put all ingredients into saucepan and cook over gentle heat
until thick, stirring well. When cool spread on dough.

Alternative filling

1 lb. cooked, sweetened and pitted prunes, mixed with
grated rind and juice of a lemon.

These cakes are peculiar to the Festival of Purim, which
occurs 4 weeks before Passover. At no other time are these
cakes made or seen in the shops.

SPONGE CAKE (1)

5 oz. castor sugar   3 oz. flour
3 eggs   ½ teaspoon baking powder

Whisk eggs and sugar until thick and creamy and practically
white. Carefully fold in flour sieved with baking powder.
Bake in two greased 7-inch sponge tins in moderate oven for
20 minutes.

SPONGE CAKE (2)

4 oz. flour	2 eggs
4 oz. sugar	4 oz. butter or margarine
½ teaspoon vanilla essence	½ teaspoon baking powder

Cream fat and sugar until thick and creamy, add eggs and beat well. Gently fold in flour sieved with baking powder, add essence. Bake in two greased 7-inch sponge tins in moderate oven for 25—30 minutes.

SPONGE CAKE (3)

| 5 oz. flour | 5 eggs |
| 6 oz. sugar | ½ teaspoon vanilla essence |

Separate whites and yolks of eggs. Beat whites until stiff, add sugar and beat for a further minute. Add yolks and beat again. Gently fold in sieved flour and essence.

Bake for 25 minutes in two 8-inch sponge tins in moderate oven.

SPONGE CAKE (4)

(Perhaps the finest of all sponge cakes, known as Genoese)

3 oz. flour	3 oz. butter (melted)
5 oz. sugar	½ teaspoon baking powder
3 eggs	

Beat eggs and sugar until very thick and creamy, practically white. Fold in alternatively butter (slightly cooled, orit may cordle eggs) and flour sieved with baking powder. Bake in moderate oven in two 7-inch tins for 25 minutes.

ALMOND TORTE

| 2 oz. flour | 6 eggs |
| 6 oz. sugar | 4 oz. ground almonds |

Separate whites and yolks of eggs. Beat whites until stiff, add sugar and beat for a further minute. Add yolks, one at a time and beat the mixture for 2 minutes. Gently and carefully fold in flour sieved with ground almonds. Bake in large greased cake tin in moderate oven for 45 minutes.

WALNUT TORTE

Proceed as for almond torte, but substitute ground walnuts for the almonds.

CHOCOLATE ALMOND TORTE

2 oz. flour	4 oz. ground almonds
6 oz. sugar	3 oz. chocolate (melted)
6 eggs	

Separate whites and yolks of eggs. Beat whites until stiff, add sugar and beat for a further minute. Add yolks, one at a time and beat the mixture for 2 minutes. Add the cooled melted chocolate and gently and carefully fold in flour sieved with the ground almonds. Bake in large greased cake tin in moderate oven for 45 minutes.

BUTTER CREAM FILLING

4 oz. butter $\frac{1}{2}$ teaspoon vanilla or
6 oz. icing sugar   lemon essence

Cream butter and sugar thoroughly together and add essence. For extra richness, add 1 beaten egg yolk.

LEMON FILLING

4 oz. butter   1 tablespoon lemon juice
6 oz. icing sugar   little grated lemon rind

Cream butter and sugar thoroughly. Add juice and rind and blend well.

ORANGE FILLING

4 oz. butter   1 tablespoon fresh orange juice
6 oz. icing sugar   little grated orange rind

Cream butter and sugar thoroughly. Add juice and rind and blend well.

CHOCOLATE FILLING

4 oz. butter $1\frac{1}{2}$ oz. melted chocolate
6 oz. icing sugar

Cream butter and sugar thoroughly. Add melted chocolate and blend well.

ALMOND FILLING

4 oz. butter $1\frac{1}{2}$ tablespoons ground almonds
6 oz. icing sugar   1 tablespoon milk

Cream butter and sugar thoroughly. Mix almonds and milk together and fold in gently, blending well with creamed mixture.

MOCHA FILLING

4 oz. butter $1\frac{1}{2}$ oz. melted chocolate
6 oz. icing sugar $\frac{1}{2}$ tablespoon coffee essence

Cream butter and sugar thoroughly. Add melted chocolate and coffee essence and mix together until well combined.

APPLE FILLING

1 lb. cooking apples   1 teaspoon lemon juice
sugar   cake crumbs

Peel, core and slice apples and cook in minimum amount of water with sugar to desired sweetness. Sieve or mash and add sufficient cake crumbs to make a firm mixture.

BANANA FILLING

2 bananas   1 teaspoon lemon juice
2 tablespoons castor sugar $\frac{1}{2}$ teaspoon grated lemon rind
1 tablespoon cream

Peel and mash bananas. Add all other ingredients and mix thoroughly.

Icing sugar must always be sieved before use.
To ice a cake. Place the cake on an upturned plate. When the icing is smooth enough and of right consistency, pour it over the centre of the cake and with a palette knife dipped in hot water smooth the icing over top and sides of cake evenly.

Butter fillings or variations of butter fillings may also be used for icing top and sides of cakes.

ALMOND PASTE (MARZIPAN)

8 oz. ground almonds   1 tablespoon lemon juice
4 oz. icing sugar   1 large egg
4 oz. castor sugar

Mix sugars and almonds and add well beaten egg and lemon juice. With the hands work to a soft dough.

GLACÉ ICING

7 oz. icing sugar   1 teaspoon desired
2 tablespoons slightly warm water   flavouring

Place sugar, water and flavouring in a bowl over hot water and stir until the mixture is just thick enough to spread.

CHOCOLATE GLACÉ ICING (1)

6 oz. icing sugar   2 tablespoons slightly warm water
1 tablespoon cocoa   1 teaspoon desired flavouring

Proceed as for glacé icing.

CHOCOLATE GLACÉ ICING (2)

Melt 1½ oz. chocolate in 2 tablespoons warm water and proceed as above.

ROYAL ICING

1 lb. icing sugar   2 teaspoons lemon juice
2 egg whites

Place sugar in a bowl. Make a small well in centre and add slightly beaten egg whites and lemon juice. Beat well until perfectly smooth.

AMERICAN ICING

1 lb. granulated sugar   2 egg whites
¼ pint water   1 teaspoon desired essence

Place the sugar and water in thick saucepan, bring slowly to the boil, and boil steadily for 7 minutes. Meanwhile, beat the egg whites to a fairly stiff froth and pour over the hot syrup. Beat or whisk until the mixture is thick enough to spread.

SMALL CAKES AND BISCUITS

The Jewish housewife always makes her weekly batch of biscuits and small cakes, and this section contains recipes of firm favourites. A store of biscuits and small cakes is a most useful standby to offer both to the expected guest for tea and to the unexpected guest for coffee.

As with recipes for large cakes, the most successful results are obtained by strictly following the instructions with regard to weight of ingredients, preparation, cooking, etc. The oven, of course, must be pre-heated to the correct temperature. The 'eye' appeal of biscuits can be enhanced by cutting them into different sizes and shapes and sets of cutters for this purpose can be purchased today very cheaply. In an emergency, a glass or cup will serve equally well.

Biscuits should be served crisp and should always be stored in an airtight tin. This should be done as soon as they are cool and if a piece of greaseproof paper is put over the tin before fitting on the lid the biscuits should remain fresh for up to 10 days.

Biscuits and cakes should never be stored together in the same tin as the biscuits will absorb moisture from the cakes and become soggy.

PARKIN

8 oz. flour
8 oz. porridge oats
4 oz. sugar
2 oz. butter or margarine

1 egg
8 oz. golden syrup
½ teaspoon bicarbonate soda
milk

Sieve flour and mix thoroughly with the oats, and add sugar. Over gentle heat in a saucepan, melt the syrup and fat and add well beaten egg. Stir well and add to the flour mixture. Dissolve bicarbonate soda in a little milk and add. If mixture is too dry a little more milk may be added if necessary. Beat mixture thoroughly for a few minutes. Turn into greased shallow tin and bake in rather hot oven for about 1 hour. When cold, cut into pieces.

NUT BUNS

3 oz. butter or margarine
3 oz. sugar
2 eggs
3 oz. chopped almonds or walnuts
extra chopped nuts

2 oz. flour
1 oz. ground rice
½ teaspoon baking
  powder
little jam

Cream fat and sugar until very thick and creamy, add well beaten eggs and beat thoroughly. Add flour sieved with baking powder and ground rice, then add nuts and combine well. Bake in small buns on greased baking sheet in hot oven for about 20 minutes. When cool, brush with a little jam if desired and roll in chopped nuts.

RASPBERRY BUNS

12 oz. flour
1 teaspoon baking powder
4 oz. butter or margarine
1 egg white

4 oz. sugar
2 eggs
raspberry jam

Cream fat and sugar and add flour sieved with baking powder. Add well beaten eggs. The mixture must be rather stiff. Place small buns on well greased tin, making a small well in each. Drop in a little jam and seal the tops of the buns. Brush over with egg white, sprinkle with a little sugar and bake in a hot oven for 15 minutes.

BRANDY SNAPS

2 oz. butter or margarine
2 oz. sugar
2 oz. flour

2 oz. golden syrup
$\frac{1}{2}$ teaspoon ground ginger
some whipped cream
(optional)

In a fairly large saucepan, over gentle heat, melt fat, syrup and sugar. Remove from heat and add flour sieved with ginger and stir thoroughly.

Drop by teaspoonfuls on a greased baking sheet, allowing room between each. Bake in hot oven until brown. While still warm roll each snap over the handle of a wooden spoon. If desired fill with whipped cream.

KRACK-A-JACK

8 oz. porridge oats
4 oz. butter or margarine
4 oz. brown sugar

1 teaspoon ratafia essence
½ teaspoon bicarbonate soda
castor sugar

In saucepan over gentle heat, melt the fat and sugar. Add oats, essence and soda dissolved in a little warm water. Bake in greased shallow tin in moderately hot oven for about 1 hour. When cool, cut into pieces and dust with castor sugar.

SHORTBREAD

4 oz. flour
4 oz. butter

2 oz. ground rice
or semolina
2 oz. sugar

With the finger tips rub the butter well in to flour sieved with ground rice or semolina, and add sugar. Work mixture on a lightly floured board until pliable. Shape into a round greased tin, about ½ inch thick. Prick the top well with a fork and pinch the edges up with the forefinger and thumb. Bake in a moderate oven for 30 minutes.

COCONUT BUNS

8 oz. flour
2 oz. butter or margarine
2 oz. castor sugar
1 egg

½ teaspoon baking powder
pinch salt
2 oz. fine desiccated coconut
milk

Cream fat and sugar until thick and creamy, add the well beaten egg, then flour sieved with baking powder, salt and coconut. Mix well together, add a little milk if necessary. Bake in small greased tins in hot oven for 10—15 minutes.

ROCK CAKES

8 oz. flour
3 oz. butter or margarine
2 oz. sugar
1 egg
milk

2 oz. currants
1 oz. finely chopped mixed
  peel
grated rind of 1 lemon
large pinch salt
$\frac{1}{2}$ teaspoon baking powder

Sieve flour, baking powder, salt and sugar. With finger tips rub in fat very finely and then add fruit, peel, and lemon rind. Mix to a stiff dough with well beaten egg and some milk if necessary. Place in small mounds on well greased baking sheet, and with the prongs of a fork make them 'rocky'. Bake in a very hot oven for 10 minutes.

BUTTER BISCUITS (KÜCHLICH)

8 oz. flour
5 oz. butter
3 oz. sugar

2 large eggs
$\frac{1}{2}$ teaspoon baking powder
pinch salt
grated rind of a lemon

Sieve flour with salt and baking powder and rub in the butter. Add sugar and combine well. Beat eggs until very light and frothy, add to mixture and then add lemon rind.

Knead and roll out to $\frac{1}{4}$ or $\frac{1}{8}$ inch in thickness as desired, cut into rounds. Place on greased baking tins and bake in moderate oven until nicely browned.

Margarine may be used instead of butter with equally successful results.

MADELEINES

4 oz. butter or margarine	4 oz. flour
4 oz. sugar	$\frac{1}{2}$ teaspoon baking powder
2 eggs	jam
glacé cherries	desiccated coconut

Cream fat and sugar and add well beaten eggs one at a time. Gently fold in flour sieved with baking powder. Fill greased dariole moulds two thirds full and bake in moderate oven for 20—25 minutes. When cool, turn out the madeleines, brush with melted jam and roll in coconut. Place half a glacé cherry on top.

Home made jam is usually made from equal parts of fruit and sugar boiled together until the mixture sets. The setting of the jam is controlled by the amount of pectin and acid in the fruit used. Some fruits contain sufficient pectin and acid so that no trouble is usually encountered in getting them to set; other fruits, particularly the favourite strawberry, contain little pectin or acid and some must always be added when making strawberry jam.

The fruit used, whatever its variety should be in perfect condition and just ripe. Over-ripe fruit loses its pectin and the results will be disappointing unless extra pectin is added.

In all cases, the fruit should be completely cooked before the sugar is added. The actual time of boiling once the sugar has been added should not be much more than 15 minutes, the jam will then retain the natural colour and flavour of its fruit.

A small piece of butter or margarine added to the boiling mixture will disperse scum which is usually formed and will prevent the jam boiling over.

Always use a large thick saucepan and fill only two thirds full, and a wooden spoon for stirring the jam during cooking.

The jam is cooked when a little placed on a cold plate sets or jellies.

All jars used should be sterilised before filling.

After potting, the jam should be covered by wax paper whilst still hot, and the top of the jar sealed, immediately. All jams should be kept in a cool, dark place.

ORANGE MARMALADE

8 Seville oranges	2 lemons
2 sweet oranges	preserving sugar

Cut fruit and extract juice. Put pith and pips in a basin, cover with cold water and leave for 24 hours. Shred peel finely, cover with water and leave this also for 24 hours, in separate basin. Put juice, shredded peel, pith and pips tied in a muslin bag and water from the two basins into saucepan. Bring to the boil and boil slowly until peel is quite soft. Remove muslin bag. Measure contents of saucepan and to every pint add 1 lb. of preserving sugar. Return to saucepan, bring to boil and stir and boil until juice jellies when tested.

Pour into dry, warm jars and seal.

STRAWBERRY JAM

2 lb. strawberries   juice of 2 lemons
(not over-ripe)   *or* commercial pectin (used as
2 lb. preserving sugar   makers' instructions)

Hull and wash fruit and place in saucepan. Add lemon juice or pectin and simmer until fruit is cooked. Add remainder of sugar and boil for 10 to 15 minutes, stirring continuously. Test on a plate. Stir jam occasionally while it is cooling. Put into warm jars and seal.

GOOSEBERRY JAM

1½ lb. gooseberries   ½ pint water
2 lb. preserving sugar

Top and tail gooseberries, wash, place in saucepan with the water and simmer until fruit is tender. Add sugar and boil for about 15 minutes, stirring continuously. Test for setting. Pour into dry, warm jars.

   Gooseberries are a good combination with strawberries for jam.

BLACKCURRANT JAM

2 lb. blackcurrants   3 lb. preserving sugar
1½ pints water

Stalk and wash fruit and place in saucepan with the water. Cook gently until fruit is absolutely tender. Add sugar and bring to the boil. Boil for about 15 minutes, stirring frequently until jam sets.

   Pour into dry, warm jars.

LEMON CURD

2 lemons   2 oz. butter
2 eggs   8 oz. castor sugar

Beat eggs and sugar in basin. Add grated rind and strained juice of lemons, and butter cut into small pieces. Place in double saucepan or in basin over boiling water and cook until mixture thickens, stirring continuously. Do not let mixture boil or it will curdle. Pour into dry, warm jars and seal.

RASPBERRY JAM

2 lb. raspberries   2 lb. sugar

Wash fruit, place in pan and cook very, very gently. Add sugar and bring to the boil, stirring continuously. Boil until jam sets.

Pour into dry, warm jars.

DAMSON JAM

2 lb. damsons $\frac{3}{4}$ pint water
2$\frac{1}{2}$ lb. preserving sugar

Wash fruit and place in saucepan with the water and cook gently until fruit is tender. Add sugar, bring to the boil and boil for about 15 minutes, stirring continuously. Test and pour into warm, dry jars.

PICKLES

Although a gourmet may regard pickles as being superfluous to good food, nevertheless, they are an established favourite with many people and their use does not reflect on the ability of the cook to produce a tasty dish.

Anyone who has had the pleasure of eating a pickled cucumber with salt beef or tongue will realise that pickles can, in the same way as a good sauce, enhance the enjoyment of a dish. Pickled gherkins and white onions, are also a very useful addition to the cocktail table.

When making pickles, use only fresh, ripe vegetables and fruit. (Over-ripe fruit and vegetables may lead to fermentation.) Use the best quality vinegar obtainable.

Pickles should not be made in copper or tin saucepans, nor should metal spoons be used for mixing. Store pickles in glass jars, making absolutely certain that the ingredients are completely covered by the vinegar.

PICKLES

SPICED VINEGAR

To each quart of water add 1 oz. of pickling spice and 1 oz. sugar. Put into an enamel saucepan, cover, bring to the boil and boil for 1 minute.

PICKLED ONIONS

Small silver onions are used for this pickle.

For easy peeling, immerse onions in boiling water for a minute or two. Drain and peel.

Place the onions in a bowl and cover with strong brine (4 oz. salt to to 2 pints water), and leave for 24 hours. Drain and place in sterilised jars. Cover with boiling spiced vinegar and seal immediately.

PICKLED CUCUMBERS

The small field cucumbers, called 'Heimische' are a favourite. They are in season about mid-July onwards for several weeks.

Wash well, and place in wide necked jars or a large bowl. Cover completely with cold brine and pickling spice and a stalk or two of dill. If a bowl is used, place a large plate on top of cucumbers and a weight on top so that the cucumbers keep completely immersed in the brine.

The cucumbers are ready when they turn yellow - about 1 week.

The small curled cucumbers called 'crooks', are also greatly relished. Procedure for pickling as above.

PICCALILLI

A combination of any of the following vegetables may be used: Cauliflower flowerettes, small pickling onions, cucumber, vegetable marrow, small green beans, gherkins. Peel onions, cut cucumber, marrow and beans into small pieces, and proceed as follows:

Sprinkle ingredients with salt and leave for 24 hours and then drain. Place vegetables in a saucepan, cover with spiced vinegar and boil gently for 15 minutes. Drain off all surplus vinegar. Add thickened vinegar and cook for 5 minutes. Put into warm jars and cover.

THICKENED VINEGAR FOR PICCALILLI

3 pints vinegar	2 oz. turmeric
3 oz. bruised mustard seed	¾ oz. flour
1 oz. ground ginger	4 oz. sugar
3 cloves bruised garlic	

Simmer all ingredients, except flour, in the vinegar for 30 minutes. When quite cold, strain, mix flour with a little of the liquid and boil all together for a few minutes.

PICKLED RED CABBAGE

1 very firm red cabbage	2 pints brown vinegar
1 oz. mixed pickling spice	salt

Trim outer leaves of cabbage, cut the cabbage into quarters and wash well. Cut out hard centre core. Shred rather finely and place in layers in a colander, salting each layer and leave for 24 hours. Boil the vinegar with the spices and leave.

Shake all moisture from the cabbage and place in jars. Pour over the vinegar and spices and tie down. The cabbage must be completely covered with the vinegar.

GREEN TOMATO CHUTNEY

3 lb. green tomatoes
1½ lb. cooking apples
2 fairly large onions
6 oz. sultanas
1 small dessertspoon salt

12 oz. brown sugar
1½ pints vinegar
½ oz. root ginger
1 tablespoon mixed pickling
  spice

Mince peeled and cored apples, peeled onions, stalked tomatoes and sultanas, and place them in a large saucepan. Add spice and ginger tied in a muslin bag and all other ingredients. Bring to boil and simmer for about 2 hours, stirring often until the chutney is pulped. Remove muslin bag. When the chutney is cold, place in jars and tie down.

TOMATO KETCHUP

3 lb. tomatoes
2 large onions
1 long seeded red
  pepper (cut)
½ clove garlic

4 oz. brown sugar
1 oz. salt
½ pint vinegar
1 tablespoon mixed
  pickling spice

Peel and slice tomatoes and onions and place them with all other ingredients in a large saucepan. (The spices should be placed in a muslin bag.) Bring to the boil and simmer for 1 hour. Remove spices and rub mixture through a sieve. Return pulp to saucepan and boil until a thin creamy consistency. Bottle, when cool, in sterilised bottle, and seal.

However fine the meal, it is seldom that one does not end it with a beverage, from the humble but nevertheless satisfying cup of tea, to coffee and liqueurs on the grander scale.

Of all the beverages, Russian Tea or Lemon Tea is, perhaps, that which is the most distinctly Jewish; it is always served after a meat meal due to the prohibition of having meat and milk dishes at the same time. For this same reason, only black coffee would be served.

As a pleasant change a fruit cordial may sometimes be served, either hot or cold, depending on the season. And on more festive occasions a glass of delicious Morella wine is sure to find an enthusiastic reception.

TEA

Always use freshly boiled water, and allow 1 teaspoon tea for every cup of boiling water. Scald the teapot and put in required amount of tea. Pour over a small amount of boiling water, cover the pot and leave to stand for a minute. Add rest of boiling water, stir tea and leave in a warm place for 2 minutes.

Of course, the amount of tea used must be according to individual taste.

RUSSIAN OR LEMON TEA

The tea is made weak, and generally served in a glass with a slice of lemon and desired amount of sugar. As tea with milk is prohibited in Jewish households after a meat meal, lemon or Russian tea is always taken.

COFFEE (1)

An old fashioned method which today still gives an excellent cup of coffee.

Place the milk or equal quantities of milk and water, (allowing a good half cup over) in a saucepan. Place on top 2 teaspoons freshly ground coffee per person (more or less according to strength of coffee required). Bring to the boil, stirring occasionally. Strain into a jug and serve.

COFFEE (2)

To make black coffee, use water only.

ICED COFFEE

This is delicious in hot weather and very simple to prepare. Chill some freshly made strong coffee. Mix with the top of the milk or a little very thin cream, but the coffee must be kept strong. Put in the refrigerator until just before serving and top with a little whipped cream.

MORELLA CHERRY WINE

Use the large black juicy Morella cherries which are obtainable about mid-July. To every pound of cherries use half a pound of castor sugar. An earthenware crock is best for making this wine, and it is a very simple process.

Put alternate layers of cherries and sugar and cork the jar, not too tightly. Leave for several months and then filter and bottle.

A quantity of brandy can be added to the cherries and sugar, and after the wine is bottled the cherries are delicious to eat.

BLACKBERRY CORDIAL

blackberries	cinnamon
sugar	nutmeg

Wash and stalk fruit and simmer until absolutely soft. Strain and measure the juice. Add 1 lb. sugar to each 2 pints of juice. Return to saucepan over a gentle heat until sugar is dissolved. Add a little cinnamon and nutmeg and simmer for 30 minutes. Pour into sterilised bottles and seal. A little of this in a glass of boiling water makes a fine hot drink in the winter.

PASSOVER COOKERY

During the Passover Festival, it is forbidden to eat or use any flour, cereals, dried peas, beans, yeast, baking powder, and in fact anything which may have come in contact, in its preparation or production, with 'leaven or chometz'. In these later years, however, many foods heretofore forbidden have been so prepared and are now sanctioned for use during this Festival, and it is now easy to have a variety of dishes.

In the orthodox home, this is the time of very thorough spring cleaning; all cooking utensils, cutlery, crockery that have been in use during the year are put away and a complete change of everything is brought out. This 'change' is put away each year and only used during this Festival.

Cooking stoves, refrigerators, are all subjected to a most intense 'spring clean'.

Any recipes in the foregoing pages that do not contain any flour or prohibited ingredients may, of course, be used, and in some recipes potato flour or fine matzo meal may be substituted.

MATZO BALLS

2 eggs
1 tablespoon chicken fat

¾ cup fine matzo meal
pinch ginger and salt to taste

Beat eggs until very frothy and add fat and seasoning. Stir in enough meal to make a fairly firm mixture, but not too dry. With hands dipped in fine meal shape mixture into balls about 1½ inches in diameter. Place in refrigerator for 1 hour, then cook in fast boiling salted water for 15 minutes. Drain well and serve in soup.

MATZO MEAL NOODLES

2 eggs
2 tablespoons fine
matzo meal

¼ teaspoon salt
little fat for frying

Beat eggs well with the salt. Add meal gradually and mix thoroughly. Melt a little fat in frying pan and when hot pour in sufficient batter to cover bottom of pan. When cooked on one side, turn and cook on the other. Roll each pancake and cut into strips about ⅛ inch wide.

Drop into boiling soup before serving.

MATZO FRY

4 matzos
little milk
2 eggs

butter or margarine
for frying
seasoning

Carefully break the matzos into equal pieces and soak them in milk, taking care not to let them get too soggy. Drain and then dip in seasoned beaten egg. Fry until crisp and brown.

MATZO MEAL PANCAKES

3 eggs   sugar or jam
1 cup fine matzo meal   salt
                           oil for frying

Into beaten yolks of the eggs stir in the matzo meal and add
a large pinch of salt. Fold in stiffly beaten egg whites and drop
by tablespoonfuls into hot oil. Fry until golden brown on
both sides. Serve with jam or sugar.

MATZO PUDDING

3 matzos   1 teaspoon cinnamon
4 oz. fine matzo meal   or mixed spice
2 eggs   4 oz. sultanas
2 oz. ground almonds   2 oz. currants
grated rind and juice of a lemon 1 teacup sugar
2 large tablespoons fat

Soak the matzos in water until soft. Squeeze very dry and
place in bowl. Add all other ingredients (except the fat) and
mix thoroughly. Melt fat in a baking dish and pour in mixture.
Bake in moderately hot oven for about 1 hour.

SCRAMBLED MATZOS

6 matzos   ½ teaspoon salt
4 eggs   butter or margarine

Soak matzos in water until very soft. Squeeze out thoroughly,
add beaten eggs and salt. Heat fat in frying pan (about
4 tablespoons) and cook as for scrambled eggs until the eggs
are just set.

MEAT PIE

1½ lb. stewing steak	*For the crust:*
1 onion	4 large potatoes
1 carrot	2 eggs
seasoning	1 tablespoon chicken fat

Cut meat into small pieces and stew until tender with the onion and carrot, cut up finely.

For the crust: Boil potatoes and when soft, mash with salt and pepper and the fat. Add 2 eggs well beaten and with this mixture line a greased pie dish. Add the meat, onion and carrot, and cover with remainder of mashed potatoes. Bake in hot oven until browned.

BEEF WITH 'SHORT' GRAVY

(Gedämpfte)

1½ lb. meat	2 large tomatoes
2 small carrots	a few mushrooms
1 medium sized onion	seasoning
matzo balls (see page 184)	1 pint water

A piece of single top rib is ideal for this recipe, otherwise stewing steak.

Place meat in cold water and bring to the boil. Skim and add prepared vegetables, seasoning and simmer until meat is tender. The meat should be barely covered with liquid, which can be thickened if desired. Serve with some matzo balls, vegetables and gravy.

VEAL WITH 'SHORT' GRAVY

(Gedämpfte)

2 lb. veal	seasoning
2 carrots	1½ pints water
1 large onion	potato flour
2 large tomatoes	

Cut meat, vegetables and tomatoes into small pieces. Place in saucepan, just covered with water, add seasoning and stew until the meat is tender. Strain and keep very hot. Thicken liquid with a little potato flour, and serve with the meat and desired vegetables.

POTATO FLOUR NOODLES

2 eggs	6 tablespoons water
1—2 oz. potato flour	little fat

Beat eggs well, add flour gradually then the water, and beat well. Melt a little fat in frying pan and when hot pour in sufficient batter to make thin pancakes. When cool, roll and cut into thin strips.

Drop into boiling soup and cook for 2 minutes.

POTATO PANCAKES

2 lb. potatoes	fine matzo meal
2 eggs	seasoning
	fat or oil for frying

Peel and grate potatoes into a bowl of cold water. Strain through muslin bag and mix in beaten eggs, seasoning and enough meal to bind.

Cook as for latkes (see page 57).

ALMOND BALLS FOR SOUP

2 oz. ground almonds	$\frac{1}{4}$ teaspoon grated lemon rind
1 egg	pinch salt

Beat egg yolk until frothy and add other ingredients. Whip the egg white until stiff and fold into mixture. Drop a little from the end a teaspoon into boiling fat and fry until golden brown. Drain well and add to soup just before serving.

TO FRY FISH

The fish is prepared as usual for frying, but it will be dipped in fine matzo meal instead of flour.

CHRIMSEL

3 matzos	$\frac{1}{4}$ teaspoon cinnamon
2 eggs	1 tablespoon ground almonds
little salt	1 tablespoon sugar
2 oz. sultana or seeded raisins	oil for frying

Soak matzos until very soft. Press out all water, place in a bowl, and mash thoroughly. Add all other ingredients, except egg whites, and mix well. Beat egg whites very stiffly and fold in. Drop by tablespoonfuls into hot oil and fry until golden brown. Serve with sugar.

COCONUT PYRAMIDS

8 oz. desiccated coconut   2 eggs (beaten)
5 oz. castor sugar

Mix all ingredients thoroughly and with wet hands form into pyramids. Place on greased baking tin and bake in moderate oven for 20 minutes, until nicely browned.

APPLE PUDDING

3 matzos
3 large cooking apples
1 cup sugar
2 oz. butter or margarine

3 eggs
$\frac{1}{2}$ teaspoon cinnamon
8 oz. raisins or sultanas,
(or mixed)

Soak matzos in water and squeeze until dry, then place them in a bowl. Peel and cut apples into thick slices and add to matzos. Then add fruit, sugar, cinnamon and well beaten eggs. Melt the fat and stir in. Adjust sweetness. Pour mixture into greased baking dish and bake in moderate oven for 45 minutes.

APPLE MERINGUE PUDDING

1 lb. cooking apples
6 oz. sugar
4 oz. fine matzo meal

3 eggs
grated rind and
juice of a lemon

Peel, core and cut apples into very small pieces. Mix with 4 oz. sugar, matzo meal, rind and juice of the lemon and beaten yolks of eggs. Turn into greased baking dish and bake in moderate oven for 35 minutes. Beat egg whites very stiffly, fold in remaining sugar and heap over pudding. Return to slow oven until the meringue is set and lightly browned.

CINNAMON BALLS

6 oz. ground almonds
8 oz. castor sugar
1 tablespoon cinnamon

3 egg whites
icing sugar
1 tablespoon fine matzo meal

Mix together in a bowl the almonds, sugar and cinnamon, add matzo meal. Beat egg whites stiffly and add sufficient only to make a paste. With wet hands roll into balls and place on greased baking sheet. Bake in fairly slow oven till set, about 25 minutes. Remove from tin and roll in icing sugar. Care must be taken to see that mixture is not too wet as the mixture will spread in the baking, but the addition of the matzo meal should prevent this.

APPLE BATTER

2 lb. cooking apples
1 cup sugar
grated peel of lemon

2 eggs
½ cup sugar
1 cup fine matzo meal

Peel, core and slice apples and cook in very little water with sugar to taste until they are just soft. Place in baking dish. Beat eggs and sugar until frothy add lemon peel and matzo meal, mixing well. Pour this batter over the apples and bake in moderately hot oven until the batter is firm and brown.

BEOLAS

6 eggs   oil for frying
6 tablespoons fine matzo meal   sugar syrup (see below)

Beat eggs until very light and frothy and fold in matzo meal.
Drop by spoonfuls into hot oil and fry until lightly browned
on both sides. Drain on paper and pour over the syrup.

Sugar Syrup

6 oz. sugar   few strips lemon rind
¼ pint water

Put ingredients in saucepan and bring to the boil. Boil for
3 or 4 minutes, leave until cold and strain.

ROUT CAKES

8 oz. ground almonds   yolks of 3 eggs
8 oz. castor sugar   icing sugar

Mix almonds and sugar well together and add sufficient of the
beaten egg yolks to form a pliable mixture. Dredge board
with icing sugar, roll out paste ⅓ inch thick and leave in a very
cool place for 1 hour. Form into any desired shapes. Place on
greased baking tin and bake in slow oven till firm.

SAND CAKE

2 oz. fine matzo meal	4 oz. potato flour
6 oz. castor sugar	3 eggs
6 oz. butter or margarine	grated rind of 1 lemon

Beat egg yolks and sugar until very frothy. Melt the butter and add, then flour, meal and lemon rind, and mix well together. Fold in stiffly beaten egg whites and turn into greased 8-inch cake tin. Bake in moderately hot oven for 1 hour.

ALMOND MACAROONS

8 oz. ground almonds	3 egg whites
8 oz. castor sugar	about 20 blanched almonds

Mix ground almonds and sugar together in bowl. Beat egg whites and add sufficient only to make a paste. If eggs are very large, two whites will be sufficient. With wet hands roll into fairly small balls and place on greased baking sheet. Flatten each macaroon with a blanched almond and bake in moderate oven for about 20 minutes until pale biscuit colour.

ALMOND BISCUITS

4 oz. ground almonds	2 oz. butter
2 oz. castor sugar	a little icing sugar
grated rind of ½ lemon	

Cream butter and sugar together, add the almonds and grated lemon rind. Knead to a pliable dough. Roll out on a board dusted with icing sugar cut into small rounds. Bake in slow oven for 20 minutes.

PASSOVER SPONGE CAKE (PLAVA)

6 eggs
8 oz castor sugar
grated rind and juice of
  lemon

4 heaped tablespoons fine
  matzo meal
2 heaped tablespoons potato
  flour

Beat yolks until very light and fluffy then fold in sugar, meal, potato flour and rind and juice of the lemon. Into the mixture carefully fold in the stiffly beaten egg whites making sure all ingredients are blended thoroughly. Pour into a greased tin lined with paper and bake in a moderate oven for 1 hour.

SOME SUGGESTIONS FOR PASSOVER MEALS

Lunches

Cream of mushroom soup (see page 29)
Cheese with matzo and butter
Salad
Sponge cake (see page 193)
Tea or coffee

Scrambled matzos (see page 185)
Fresh or stewed fruit
Cheese with matzo and butter
Tea or coffee

Gefillte fish with horseradish sauce (see pages 50, 109)
Chrimsel (see page 188)
Cake and/or biscuits
Tea or coffee

Stewed or fried fish
Salad
Matzo and butter
Stewed fruit
Tea or coffee

Cream of asparagus soup (see page 29)
Matzo meal pancakes (see page 185)
Cheese and tomatoes
Cake and/or biscuits
Tea or coffee

Dinners

Chopped liver
Bortsch (see page 32)
Roast chicken (see page 82)
Brussels sprouts
Boiled potatoes
Compote of fruit
Black coffee or Russian tea

Eggs and onions
Lamb chops
Mashed potatoes
Cauliflower
Matzo pudding (see page 185)
Black coffee or Russian tea (see pages 180, 181)

Grapefruit
Boiled salmon (see page 52)
Salad
Boiled potatoes
Sponge cake and cookies (see pages 193, 192)
Tea or coffee

Grapefruit
Chicken soup with Kneid-
   lech (see pages 26, 37)
Roast veal (see page 68)
Baked potatoes
Brussels sprouts
Fresh fruit
Black coffee or Russian tea

Mixed hors-d'oeuvre
Grilled steak (see page 66)
Boiled potatoes (see page
   56)
Salad
Apple pudding (see page
   189)
Black Coffee or Russian
   tea

SOME SUGGESTIONS FOR JEWISH FESTIVAL MEALS

New Year (Rosh Ha Shanah). After the customary blessing over the bread, it is dipped into honey instead of salt. A small piece of apple dipped in honey is also eaten and it is also the practice to serve some fruit that has not yet been eaten during that year.

Lunch

Grapefruit
Gefillte or Fried Fish (see pages 50, 40)
Salad
Honey cake (see page 157)
Tea or coffee

Dinner

Melon
Chicken soup with vermicelli and small
   mincemeat balls (see pages 35, 71)
Boiled or roast chicken, vegetables (see page 82)
Strudel
Russian tea or black coffee (see page 193, 192)

Eve of the Day of Atonement (Erev Yom Kippur). To avoid thirst, no highly spiced or seasoned dishes are partaken as this meal precedes the Fast.

Dinner

> Melon or Grapefruit
> Chicken Soup with Kreplach or Rice or Vermicelli
> (see pages 26, 36, 38, 27)
> Chicken or Meat with boiled potatoes, peas
> Tzimmis (see page 60) *or*
> Stewed Prunes *or*
> Fresh Fruit
> Russian Tea or Black Coffee (see page 193, 192)

The Harvest Festival (Succoth). No special dishes are served, but Stuffed Cabbage (see page 59), is generally included on the dinner menu.

The Festival of Lights (Chanukah). The only traditional dish served is 'Latkes' (see page 57).

The Feast of Esther (Purim). As nice a meal as possible is served. The Hamantaschen cakes (see page 158) are an item on the tea menu as they are made with milk.

The Passover (Pesach). See separate sections (pages 183, 193).

Pentecost (Shevuoth). It is customary to serve milk dishes and dishes made from dairy products, e.g. Cream Soups, Fish, Cheese Cake, Cheese Blintzes, Fruit Salads, new vegetables in season, Salads, Coffee, etc.

INDEX OF RECIPES